TOP
50
Popular
Modern
Coins

Comprehensive Guide to the Most
Sought After U.S. Issues (1986-Date)

ERIC JORDAN
JOHN MABEN

Published by

Krause Publications, a division of F+W Media, Inc.
700 East State Street • Iola, WI 54990-0001
715-445-2214 • 888-457-2873
www.krausebooks.com

To order books or other products call toll-free 1-800-258-0929
or visit us online at www.shopnumismaster.com

ISBN-13: 978-1-4402-3067-7
ISBN-10: 1-4402-3067-6

Cover Design by Chuck Daughtrey
Designed by Chuck Daughtrey
Edited by Debbie Bradley

Printed in China

Table of Contents

Foreword

By Mark Salzberg, Chairman
Numismatic Guaranty Corporation

The revival of commemorative coinage that began with the Washington half dollar in 1982 breathed new life into the collecting of current or recent U. S. coins, an area that had been dormant for years after the introduction of clad coinage in 1965.

The market for modern United States coins has exploded since then, offering the current generation of coin enthusiasts an affordable avenue for building an attractive and interesting collection. This growth in popularity has gone hand-in-hand with the rise of online collecting sites such as the Numismatic Guaranty Corporation Coin Registry. Collectors cannot only enjoy the coins themselves, but they can also share their accomplishments with like-minded coin buyers and match their collections against those of other NGC Registry participants.

Authors Eric Jordan and John Maben have put together a terrific little book that identifies and describes the 50 most popular modern coins in today's hobby. Their years of experience as leaders in the modern coin market have given them the insight needed to determine which coins are the ones most often sought by collectors. While some issues may be more rare or more valuable than the ones in this book, the 50 entries included in these pages are the ones that collectors truly want. They're the coins with the most attractive designs and the most important subjects that really grab a collector's attention.

I compare the appeal of these modern coins to post-war or pop art and the explosion of popularity in that field. The collectors in those areas simply love the art and happen to have the money to buy it, not dwelling on the historical value of paintings that may be from 50 or 100 years earlier.

Top 50 Most Popular Modern Coins has everything you'll need to make the most of your collecting experience. In addition to great photos showing both sides of each coin, you'll find a price guide for all entries as "raw," or uncertified coins, as well as their values in the NGC-certified grades of MS-69 and MS-70, the ones most highly sought by collectors of modern coins. There are mintage figures for both the Top 50 entries and hundreds of other widely collected modern coins.

I'm so pleased with what Eric and John have accomplished that NGC has created a unique grading label for the Top 50 Most Popular Modern Coins. When you submit any one of these coins for NGC certification, it will be eligible for this special label identifying it as a Top 50 entry. NGC has also created a new Registry Set for the Top 50 where collectors can share their accomplishments and compete against other participants for highest scores.

Collecting modern coins is fun. Thanks to the fine work of Eric Jordan and John Maben, it is now also something that can be done with a real sense of direction. Their book provides an all-you-need guide to smart collecting, and its handy size means that you can always have it with you at coin shows. This is the must-have book for the modern coin collector.

Mark Salzberg is the chairman of Numismatic Guaranty Corporation (NGC), the world's largest third-party coin grading service. A lifelong numismatist, Mark has personally graded nearly all of the significant rarities and collections to come to market in the past 25 years. Mark is widely recognized for his grading expertise and is a central figure in promoting coin certification both in the United States and abroad.

In recognition of his achievements, the American Numismatic Association gave Mark the ANA Presidential Award in 1998 and named him Numismatist of the Year in 2006. Mark continues to give back to the industry through his sponsorship of the Smithsonian's Legendary Coins & Currency exhibit and support of the American Numismatic Association.

Acknowledgments

"I would like to take this opportunity to thank my wife Wendy Jo for putting up with the endless hours of studying to complete this text, my parents Buck and Sandy Jordan, my grandparents Bob and Nora Rice, and my brother Brian's family for their love and support. Most of all I would like to thank Jesus for His unfailing love and mercy."

— Eric Jordan

"I'd like to thank my original numismatic mentors Steve Paradisi and Frank Greenberg for introducing me to coins and educating me, and my parents Jack and Alice Maben for their love, support, and encouragement which continue to this day".

— John Maben

John and Eric would like to give a "special thanks" to Jay Rudo, Richard Lecce, Chuck Daughtrey, and Numismatic Guaranty Corporation for their support and contributions.

A Word from the Authors

By Eric Jordan

What coin being produced today will turn into a coveted rarity 20 years from now? If only we had a crystal ball to reveal the coins of today that will be the rarities of tomorrow.

What we do know is that since 1986 the U.S. Mint has been actively producing attractive coin series struck on silver, gold and platinum that are rapidly acquiring an enthusiastic collector following. Many modern Eagles enjoy rarity on a scale not seen in 100 years and many are still affordable.

Today collectors can assemble a great collection on a limited budget if they have a willingness to cherrypick coins issued today. Most of the coins included here are attractive keys to rapidly growing series, amazingly rare type coins with mintages as low as 2,200 and cohesive short sets. And, most of the issues are struck on precious metals, thus creating a protective value floor for their holdings if something should happen to the collector markets.

In this book, and its forerunner, *Modern Commemorative Coins*, we have gone to great lengths to present accurate mintage figures with the help of the U.S. Mint's Office of Public Affairs. This is a wonderful and exciting time to be a collector of modern United States coins.

By John Maben

When I left professional grading in 2004 to resume my career as a coin dealer, I took a long, hard look at the numismatic market as a whole. The classic coin market had its place, but was largely overpopulated. I didn't really see much activity (at the time) in paper money as compared to coins. World coins definitely were intriguing, but the older coins were a highly specialized area and the modern issues were only in the very early stages of matura- tion. After a few months of dealing in classic coins, I considered modern coins and the idea stuck with me, so I adjusted my business model leaning heavily on the purchase and sale of coins minted 1982 and after.

I had no idea at the time that the demand could lead us to become one of the largest discount retailers for modern coins in the world. It is the wealth of experience I gained in the modern coin market that led me to publish this work. I believe the modern coin market is largely untapped with a lot of potential for collectors to be able to purchase a number of relatively scarce issues at very reasonable prices from a variety of sources.

This book should serve to allow you to see into the world of a dealer who buys and sells a large number of modern coins on a very regular basis. I spend a majority of my waking hours with modern coins, and know through experience which of the modern issues are challenging yet obtainable, desired by many, and are reasonably priced with regard to their relative scarcity and popularity among collectors. Having a comprehensive understanding of this information is paramount to assembling a challenging and rewarding collection of modern coins.

How to Use this Book

Purpose of this book:
To assist the collector in understanding which issues in modern coins are the top collectible choices across the modern coin market with regard to three main factors:

1. The popularity of the issue as compared to other similar issues and the modern coin market as a whole.
2. The scarcity of the issue in relative terms to other similar issues and the urgency to obtain them when they become available.
3. The affordability of the issue considering the other two factors listed above.

A word to collectors: First and foremost, collect what you LIKE. This book is NOT intended to tell you what to collect if you already have direction in your collection. It is more intended to assist those who have just met a goal in collecting and are looking for additional direction, or those who might be inexperienced and are looking for direction. By all means do not change what you collect if you are enjoying your hobby simply based on the advice given in this writing. We stress that collecting should be fun – a challenge that has the reward of 'completeness' when finished. For that reason, we did not include any issues in this book that are one-of-a-kind, and very few that are so rare they seldom come to market. We also chose to include very few issues that are so expensive as to be relatively unaffordable to most collectors. Every issue listed in this book, while some may be expensive, are obtainable within a realistic period of time at a reasonable budget level.

The factors listed for each issue:
All three factors for each issue are comparing that issue to other very similar issues. For instance, the 2004-W Proof Platinum Eagle issues listed herein are assigned factors as compared to other Proof Platinum issues – not to unrelated issues such as the 2006-W Burnished Mint State Silver Eagles. Each factor is assigned by the authors based on years of experience completely immersed in the market. They are not scientifically derived from computer generated algorithms. The 'overall score' for each issue, however, is a mathematical average of the other three factors, and is meant to give the collector a 'greater scope' insight as to which issues might be more or less difficult to obtain or purchase on a limited budget.

Each factor is meant to answer a specific question in a ranking from one (1) to five (5) in half-point increments. The questions these factors answer are:

1. **Popularity:** About how many collectors, on average, out of a given number would want this issue in their collection to serve as a part of the goal of their collection? A factor of one (1) would mean that the issue is not a commonly collected issue for most collectors. A factor of five (5) would mean that most collectors would want this issue to serve the needs of their collecting goal.
2. **Scarcity:** Of the total number of collectors who would want this issue to complete their collecting goals, how many exist? A factor of one (1) means there are plenty to go around. A factor of five (5) means there were not enough coins minted to serve the demand of all the collectors who would want this issue to fill their collecting goals.
3. **Affordability:** Compared to other like issues, how reasonably priced is this particular issue? A factor of one (1) means this issue is very inexpensive as compared to other like issues. A factor of five (5) means this issue is quite expensive as compared to other like issues.

The order of coins in this book:
Every list must have an order; without knowing the reason for a list's order, the purpose of the list can sometimes be completely misunderstood. This book is NOT compiled as a top-down list with the most popular issue first. We do not believe it is fair to compare these issues with each other in this fashion. Instead, this book is assembled in issue order as most guides would logically order the issues with thought given only to date, series, and denomination.

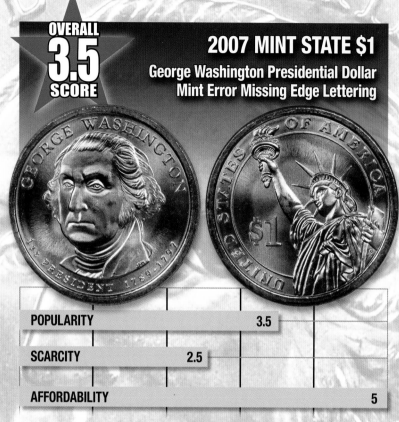

OVERALL 3.5 SCORE

2007 MINT STATE $1
George Washington Presidential Dollar
Mint Error Missing Edge Lettering

POPULARITY			3.5	
SCARCITY		2.5		
AFFORDABILITY				5

STATISTICAL INFORMATION

Mintage: unknown

Obverse Designer: Joseph Menna

Reverse Designer: Don Everhart

Diameter: 26.5 mm

Weight: 8.1 grams

Composition: .770 copper, .120 zinc, .070 manganese, .040 nickel

AGW: N/A

Lettered Edge Type: plain

ESTIMATED RETAIL VALUE

UNCERTIFIED	NGC MS66	NGC MS67
$75	$125	$895

2007 Mint State $1
George Washington Presidential Dollar
Mint Error Missing Edge Lettering

One of the primary themes of this text is the concept that coins are rarely great in their own right. They are great in the context of the series in which they inhabit.

What makes a series great? Great series tend to have many common dates that help us get our sets started. The designs and themes portrayed need to speak to us, but if a series or coin is just good looking and dirt common it will never have a great collector following because we also like a challenge.

Series need a few rare or scarce issues in their midst in order to go on to greatness. Rarity more often than not is the child of a production related constraint, economic distortion or rejection by the collecting public in the year of issue or soon after. In short, they are troubled young coins that go on to become numismatic royalty in the midst of their series as they age.

The Presidential dollars are a perfect illustration of these concepts. Following on the heels of the stunning success of the 50 State Quarters Program, there was support in Congress for the creation of a circulating series with one side highlighting the presidents. It looked like an excellent idea on the surface. There were thought to be 100 million State quarters collectors, and the government was doing very well selling quarters to the public at a 17-cent profit on every coin struck. The Presidential dollars stood the chance of making 80 cents per coin struck, and if the coin replaced the costly and short-life dollar bill to any extent, it was the best of both worlds.

The economic distress of 2008 was the first nail in this plan's coffin. The dollars that were struck either returned to the Federal Reserve in mass or never left at all. Just as the Great Depression created the ultra low mintages seen in the early 1930s, so too mintages of the Presidential dollars have crashed and there is pressure to make them special issue coins sold only to collectors until the bloated inventory situation improves. In either case, this historically interesting series is picking up noteworthy key dates precisely because of serious troubled infancy issues.

The edge lettering on these coins has proved to be a quality control problem for the Mint and offers an opportunity for the collectors. It's easy for a small percentage of the Presidential dollars to make it out the door with the lettering missing, and this was the case with the very first Issue. George Washington smooth edge dollars with missing edge lettering have been very popular with collectors since they were first discovered. Its inclusion is a tribute to the many interesting things that are going on with this series, whose tale of success and hardship have only begun to be told.

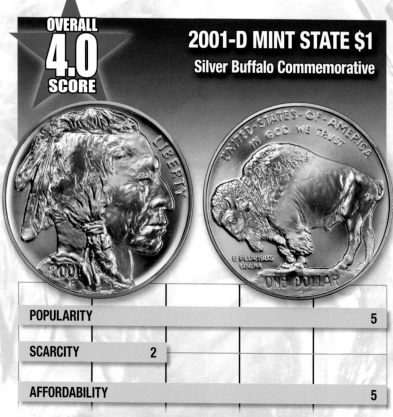

2001-D MINT STATE $1
Silver Buffalo Commemorative

POPULARITY		5
SCARCITY	2	
AFFORDABILITY		5

STATISTICAL INFORMATION

Mintage: 227,131

Obverse Designer: James Earle Fraser

Reverse Designer: James Earle Fraser

Diameter: 38.1 mm

Weight: 26.73 grams

Composition: .900 silver

ASW: .7736 oz.

Edge Type: reeded

ESTIMATED RETAIL VALUE

UNCERTIFIED	NGC MS69	NGC MS70
$180	$190	$450

2001-D Mint State $1
Silver Buffalo Commemorative

The Buffalo silver dollar commemorative was one of the programs recommended in a Citizen Commemorative Coin Advisory Committee five-year plan. One of the major points it made to Congress after the collapse of the commemorative market in the mid-1990s was that coin collectors are attracted to classic and iconic designs and that programs need to incorporate them in order to be successful.

The selection of the old Type I Buffalo nickel design for a silver dollar commemorative design was a stroke of marketing genius, and it produced marvelous results.

The issue was developed to commemorate the opening of the National Museum of the American Indian of the Smithsonian Institution and supplement its endowment and educational outreach funds. A maximum mintage of 500,000 proof and mint state dollars was called for, and in marked departure from recent sales trends, the coins sold out.

The mint state silver Buffalo has enjoyed fantastic popularity over the last 10 years. Many commemorative collectors don't feel locked into a tight set structure, so they tend to do what works for them. That means buy what they like and pass over the rest of the coins in the series that don't inspire them.

The mint state silver Buffalo is not only an important coin to silver commemorative collectors, it's also a desirable and affordable part of the modern Buffalo type set.

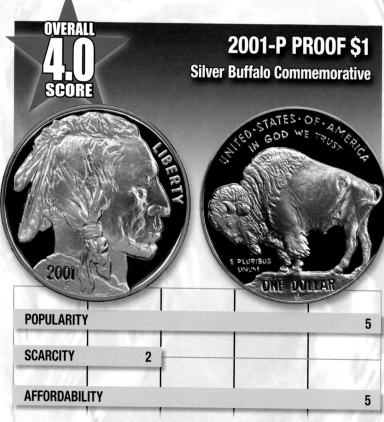

2001-P PROOF $1
Silver Buffalo Commemorative

OVERALL 4.0 SCORE

POPULARITY				5
SCARCITY	2			
AFFORDABILITY				5

STATISTICAL INFORMATION

Mintage: 272,869

Obverse Designer: James Earle Fraser

Reverse Designer: James Earle Fraser

Diameter: 38.1 mm

Weight: 26.73 grams

Composition: .900 silver

ASW: .7736 oz.

Edge Type: reeded

ESTIMATED RETAIL VALUE

UNCERTIFIED	NGC PF69 UC	NGC PF70 UC
$185	$200	$850

2001-P Proof $1
Silver Buffalo Commemorative

The Buffalo commemorative dollar is a case study on how series without consistent design elements behave. With its 272,869 mintage it is one of the more common proof silver dollar commemoratives, but it's also the most expensive.

Series with a consistent design element create a very clear set that has cohesion among its members, and the most expensive is almost always the rarest. Many commemoratives are not priced based on which coin in the set is the rarest, but how popular the particular design is relative to its mintage.

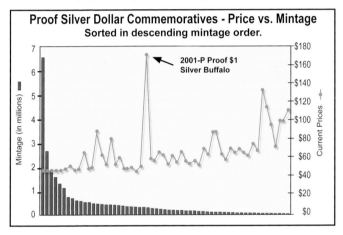

The proof Buffalo dollar is acting like it is a low mintage competitor to the Silver Eagle. Below is the mintage vs. price trend line for proof Silver Eagles with the Buffalo proof thrown in. It's amazing how well the Buffalo proof fits the price trend line of Silver Eagles for its mintage, which is shown in red. Obviously the size and quality of the collector groups perusing these coins are similar.

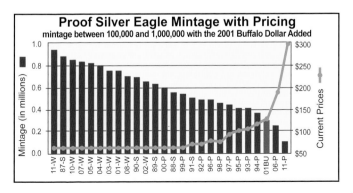

OVERALL 3.5 SCORE

1997-W MINT STATE $5 GOLD
Jackie Robinson Commemorative

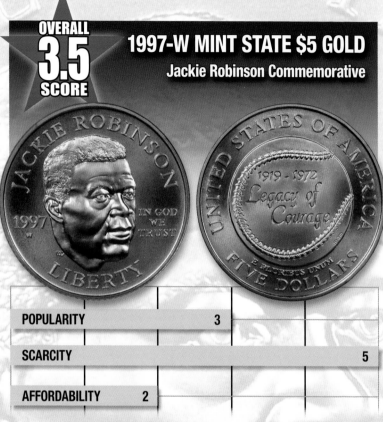

POPULARITY	3		
SCARCITY			5
AFFORDABILITY	2		

STATISTICAL INFORMATION

Mintage: 5,174

Obverse Designer: William C. Cousins

Reverse Designer: James M. Peed

Diameter: 21.6 mm

Weight: 8.359 grams

Composition: .900 gold

AGW: .242 oz.

Edge Type: reeded

ESTIMATED RETAIL VALUE

UNCERTIFIED	NGC MS69	NGC MS70
$3,000	$3,100	$4,500

1997-W Mint State $5 Gold
Jackie Robinson Commemorative

The history of the mint state Jackie Robinson, as collectors refer to it, has volumes to teach us about modern coins in general.

When the U.S. Mint first started issuing gold commemoratives in the 1980s after a 58-year hiatus, the collecting public was thrilled. Combined mint state and proof sales for commemorative gold, regardless of denomination, were in the 500,000-coin range and stayed there until 1988 when market saturation started to take place.

By 1990, the after-market price for new $5 issues was falling back to melt value or less, quickly discouraging the next round of purchases by the public. It was better to hold off and buy the coins you liked after the price had some time to settle. Mintages for mint state commemoratives dropped from 214,000 in 1987 to 22,000 by 1996.

Starting in 1995, a half dozen proof and mint state $5 gold commemoratives were offered to the public as prescribed by Congress, and what little demand there was for the coins was splintered. Collectors were already cost weary and mintages crashed by 50 percent in one year. The same thing happened in 1996 and mintages fell into the 9,000 range for the 1996-dated Olympic gold.

Between the "buy it cheaper after sales closure" mindset and the collector fatigue of too many issues in the last 24 months, the stage was set for Jackie Robinson. The mint state version was not particularly lovely and it just did not sell, giving Jackie a new mintage low for a modern coin of 5,174. Starting the following year, mintages by and large moved back into the 10,000 to 20,000 range and a bottom was formed.

Mint state Jackie Robinson reigned as the lowest mintage modern coin struck on a precious metal from 1997 to 2004, and during that period major market makers and promoters took notice and began the long process of promoting the coin. It moved from less than $300 in 1997 to almost $5,000 a dozen years later.

Today it is nowhere close to being the rarest modern, but it is the rarest $5 gold commemorative by a wide margin and well liked by collectors. Recently promoters who once drove the coin past its fair market MS-69 value based on mintage have exited the scene and its price has settled back to levels that more accurately reflect fundamental collector and mintage relationships.

1997-W PROOF $5 GOLD
Jackie Robinson Commemorative

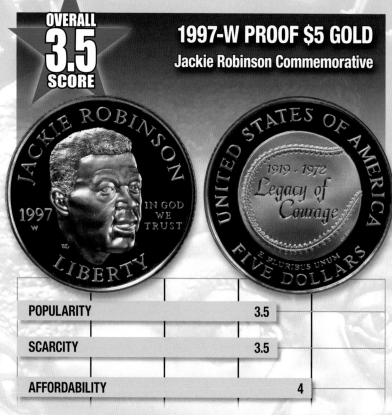

POPULARITY	3.5
SCARCITY	3.5
AFFORDABILITY	4

STATISTICAL INFORMATION

Mintage: 24,072

Obverse Designer: William C. Cousins

Reverse Designer: James M. Peed

Diameter: 21.6 mm

Weight: 8.359 grams

Composition: .900 gold

AGW: .242 oz.

Edge Type: reeded

ESTIMATED RETAIL VALUE

UNCERTIFIED	NGC PF69 UC	NGC PF70 UC
$600	$650	$1,600

1997-W Proof $5 Gold
Jackie Robinson Commemorative

The 1997-W proof $5 gold Jackie Robinson commemorative coin was issued to mark the 60th anniversary of his Major League debut and to honor his efforts as a civil rights leader.

The obverse depicts Robinson in his later years as a civil rights activist, while the reverse marks the years of his life from 1919 to 1972. His life is described as a "Legacy of Courage." The surcharges for the program were paid to the Jackie Robinson Foundation to support educational and leadership programs and scholarships.

This proof has one of the lower mintages in the $5 gold commemorative series at 24,072 coins. Given the drop in late 1990s mintages, that's reasonable. The much harder question is why did the proof issue sell 4.65 times as many coins as the mint state issue? This was the largest proof vs. mint state sales percentage divergence for any $5 gold commemorative of any year.

A special "Legacy Set" that included the $5 proof gold commemorative coin with a baseball card, pin, and patch was the likely culprit of this divergence. The special baseball card was scarce; only issued in these sets, it created its own rarity market in the sports memorabilia scene.

Today the proof Jackie Robinson is one of the more expensive issues of its series even though it is not the rarest. Part of the reason for the higher price on this coin is the halo effect it receives from the outstanding rarity and resulting market value of its mint state sibling. Those who would like a representative example but can't afford a mint state coin just buy the proof as an attractive substitute.

1997 Jackie Robinson 'Legacy Set' included the $5 gold commemorative, a card, a pin and a patch in a solid wood display box.

2000-W MINT STATE $10
Bimetallic Library of Congress Commemorative

POPULARITY	3		
SCARCITY		4	
AFFORDABILITY	2		

STATISTICAL INFORMATION

Mintage: 6,683

Obverse Designer: John Mercanti

Reverse Designer: Thomas D. Rogers Sr.

Diameter: 27 mm

Weight: 16.259 grams

Composition: .480 gold, .480 platinum, .04 alloy

AGW: 0.28 oz.   **APW:** 0.28 oz.

Edge Type: reeded

ESTIMATED RETAIL VALUE

UNCERTIFIED	NGC MS69	NGC MS70
$4,000	$4,100	$5,250

2000-W Mint State $10 Bimetallic Library of Congress Commemorative

The 2000-W mint state $10 bimetillic Library of Congress commemorative in its year of issue was greeted with a cool reception and only 6,683 coins sold.

The Mint had expected this coin to sell very well. Ringed bimetallics had been popular in Europe for many years, and the year 2000 represented a millennial turn. Even the enabling legislation set an optimistic bimetallic sales limit of 200,000 coins.

The problem was that coins are normally great in the context of the set in which they inhabit. The $10 commemorative production has been extremely sporadic over the years, and it has hampered the development of a strong collector following. As usual, initial rejection by the collecting public set the stage for the eventual greatness that we see today. The three members of the $10 modern commemoratives are shown below with their respective mintages.

Mints State $10 Modern Commemoratives	Mintage
1984-W Los Angeles Olympiad Gold	75,886
2000-W Library of Congress Bimetallic	6,683
2003-W First Flight Gold	10,129

Normally large and popular series with a significant number of members build the kind of collector followings that drive the rarest issue in a set to amazing heights. Obviously this set has very few members and low total series population so something else has made the bimetallic pull so hard so quickly.

One of the best guides to understanding modern issues and where they are in their development cycle is to look at the behavior of similar coins that have had time to fully mature. The 1915 Panama Pacific $2.5 gold commemorative with its 6,749 mintage has almost exactly the same initial population as the bimetallic and its price looks a lot like the small Pan Pac's $4,000 typical mint state price after 100 years of growth! The mint state bimetallic managed to pick up 100 years worth of price development in 10 years because it has been promoted by strong marketers who have focused on its unique characteristics. That has driven it into price maturity prematurely.

The reasoning for this coin's stellar performance over the last decade is straightforward. It's the only mint state bimetallic ever struck by the U.S. Mint, the coin's design is attractive, its date is a millennial turn and its mintage is low enough to make cornering the market through promotions an achievable task.

2000-W PROOF $10
Bimetallic Library of Congress Commemorative

POPULARITY	3	
SCARCITY		4
AFFORDABILITY	2	

STATISTICAL INFORMATION

Mintage: 27,167

Obverse Designer: John Mercanti

Reverse Designer: Thomas D. Rogers Sr.

Diameter: 27 mm

Weight: 16.259 grams

Composition: .480 gold, .480 platinum, .04 alloy

AGW: 0.28 oz.   **APW:** 0.28 oz.

Edge Type: reeded

ESTIMATED RETAIL VALUE

UNCERTIFIED	NGC PF69 UC	NGC PF70 UC
$1,250	$1,350	$2,200

2000-W Proof $10 Bimetallic Library of Congress Commemorative

This $10 bimetallic commemorative was struck to mark the 200th anniversary of the Library of Congress, the oldest federal cultural institution and the largest library in the world.

It's a beautiful bimetallic coin composed of an inner core of platinum encircled by an outer ring of gold. The outer ring was stamped from a sheet of gold and then a solid core of platinum was placed within the ring. The gold ring and platinum core were then simultaneously struck forming an annular bead where the two precious metals meet.

John Mercanti, who was later named the 12th chief engraver for the U.S. Mint, designed the obverse. It consists of the hand of Minerva, the mythical Goddess of wisdom, raising the torch of learning over the dome of the library's Jefferson Building that was built in 1897. Thomas Jefferson played an important role in the library's development. He sold his personal collection of 6,487 books, which was considered one of the finest and most extensive in the country, to the library after the British burned the Capital and library in 1814.

The reverse was designed by Thomas Rogers. It contains the stylized eagle that has served as the logo of the Library of Congress since World War II, encircled by a laurel wreath symbolizing national accomplishment.

The proof and mint state bimetallics issued along with companion silver dollars and a 33-cent stamp from the U.S. Postal Service were intended to increase the library's visibility throughout the nation and produce revenue to fund its outreach programs. As the first commemorative of the new millennium, the coin sold reasonably well in proof form with a final mintage of 27,167.

The proof bimetallic is not the rarest issue in the short $10 modern commemorative set, but it is easily the most expensive due to its unique characteristics that make it one of the more popular modern issues.

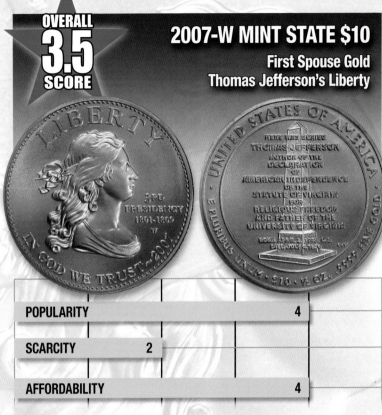

OVERALL
3.5
SCORE

2007-W MINT STATE $10
First Spouse Gold
Thomas Jefferson's Liberty

POPULARITY		4	
SCARCITY	2		
AFFORDABILITY		4	

STATISTICAL INFORMATION

Mintage: 19,823

Obverse Designer: Phebe Hemphill

Reverse Designer: Charles Vickers

Diameter: 26.49 mm

Weight: 15.554 grams

Composition: .9999 gold

AGW: .5 oz.

Edge Type: reeded

ESTIMATED RETAIL VALUE

UNCERTIFIED	NGC MS69	NGC MS70
$1,000	$1,025	$1,125

2007-W Mint State $10 First Spouse Gold Thomas Jefferson's Liberty

Thomas Jefferson's Draped Bust Liberty is the highest mintage First Spouse mint state gold coin ever struck.

The initial enthusiasm that the public frequently has for new issues (often referred to as the inaugural sales spike) was intense for the first three First Spouse gold issues, but when the after-market price for the coins crashed soon after they were offered many coins with outstanding return options were exercised. Very few of the good looking mint state Jeffersons were returned because they were so well liked, leaving them the high water mark with a 19,823 mintage.

It's hard to know exactly how many of these .9999 fine gold coins still exist. Gold bars and Gold Eagles carry a slight premium over melt as the price of gold marches upward, but these coins are not a recognized standard in gold markets, so 2007-dated First Spouse issues have frequently traded at a discount to their metal content. Large metal traders that make their own bars bought thousands of the early issues for less than their gold melt value and formed them into gold bars.

> ## LIBERTY GOLD SUBSET
>
> The First Spouse gold coins honoring Thomas Jefferson, Andrew Jackson, Martin Van Buren and and James Buchanan are known as the Liberty gold subset.
>
> The designs depicted on the four coins were the appearance of "Liberty" on circulating coinage during the presidency periods for each of the presidents they represent.
>
> The featured Liberty designs are:
> 1. Jefferson – Draped Bust Liberty
> 2. Jackson – Capped Bust Liberty
> 3. Van Buren – Seated Liberty
> 4. Buchanan – Coronet Liberty

One of the best things that can happen to a series is to have a large population of good looking common dates in the hands of the public to get them started without the intimidating hurdle of a high collector premium. Jefferson's Liberty is this coin to the four-coin Liberty gold subset. The Draped Bust Liberty obverse and Jefferson's epitaph listing his noteworthy life's contributions to the nation and his native Virginia on the reverse is a combination that collectors can appreciate and relate to. Many collectors feel that this coin is the epitome of what this series should have been, gorgeous and historically relevant.

For collectors who would like to own a well-struck example of a Draped Bust coin in a perfect state of preservation or for those who would like to complete the mint state Liberty subset, this coin is a prized addition to their collection.

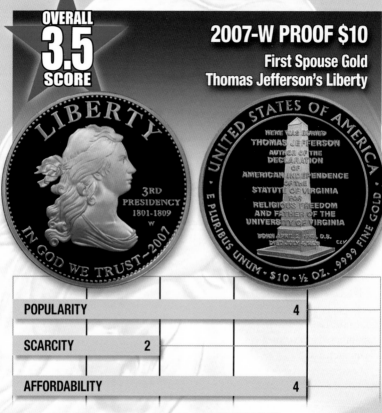

2007-W PROOF $10
First Spouse Gold
Thomas Jefferson's Liberty

POPULARITY		4
SCARCITY	2	
AFFORDABILITY		4

STATISTICAL INFORMATION

Mintage: 19,815

Obverse Designer: Phebe Hemphill

Reverse Designer: Charles Vickers

Diameter: 26.49 mm

Weight: 15.554 grams

Composition: .9999 gold

AGW: .5 oz.

Edge Type: reeded

ESTIMATED RETAIL VALUE

UNCERTIFIED	NGC PF69 UC	NGC PF70 UC
$1,025	$1,050	$1,175

2007-W Proof $10 First Spouse Gold Thomas Jefferson's Liberty

The Presidential $1 Coin Act of 2005 that created the First Spouse series required that in the event a president served without a spouse, an image of Liberty used on coinage while he was in office would be used as the obverse, and a theme representative of his life's accomplishments would appear on the reverse.

The image selected for this coin's obverse originally appeared on the Draped Bust half cent from 1800 to 1808, almost exactly the same timeframe as Jefferson was president.

The reverse side shows Thomas Jefferson's' monument inscribed with his epitaph that is located on the grounds of Monticello. It reads, "Here was buried Thomas Jefferson, Author of the Declaration of Independence, of the Statute of Virginia for Religious Freedom, and Father of the University of Virginia." It is justifiably considered by many to be one of the best looking and historically fitting issues in the entire series.

The public's approval of the coin even shows up in the final mintage charts. The first three First Spouse gold issues all sold out to the 20,000 maximum sales limit imposed by the Mint's marketing department, but quite a few of the 2007 Washington and Adams coins were sent back because the after-market price for the coins collapsed soon after issue. Not so for the Jefferson. It sold out the 20,000-coin limit, and poor after-market or not, almost all of the coins stayed in the hands of the public. This coin has the highest final mintage of any proof gold issue in its series.

If it's true that good looking high mintage common dates with mild prices floating around in the hands of the public are silent advertisements encouraging people to start working on a set, then the four-coin set with the old Liberty obverses is blessed to have this coin as its introduction.

This coin is not just appealing to moderns collectors, it also offers a special opportunity to collectors of early 1800s U.S. coinage. Where else can you acquire an early bust design struck as a cameo proof with razor sharp detail that is completely free of bag marks? The answer is nowhere.

OVERALL 3.5 SCORE

2008-W MINT STATE $10
First Spouse Gold
Andrew Jackson's Liberty

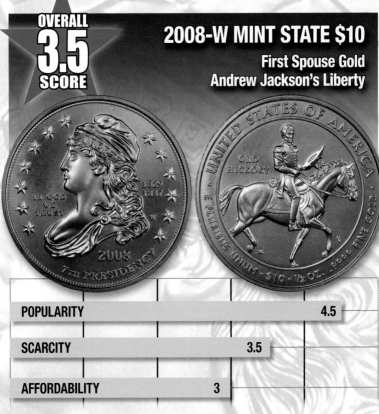

POPULARITY				4.5
SCARCITY			3.5	
AFFORDABILITY		3		

STATISTICAL INFORMATION

Mintage: 4,609

Obverse Designer: John Reich

Reverse Designer: Justin Kunz

Diameter: 26.49 mm

Weight: 15.554 grams

Composition: .9999 gold

AGW: .5 oz.

Edge Type: reeded

ESTIMATED RETAIL VALUE

UNCERTIFIED	NGC MS69	NGC MS70
$1,600	$1,650	$2,100

2008-W Mint State $10 First Spouse Gold Andrew Jackson's Liberty

Andrew Jackson's Capped Bust Liberty, the second coin in the Liberty gold subset, is well liked and getting harder to find for many reasons.

This coin was not a favorite of speculators in its year of issue, so most of them were purchased by small volume buyers that are more likely to buy and hold than buy and sell. The lack of initial dealer/speculator interest also contributed to the coin's very favorable 4,609 final mintage.

It normally takes up to four years for market inventories of new issues to become depleted, but once that happens coins that enjoy continuing collector interest start to show enduring strength. This coin is a prime example of a slightly overlooked attractive modern coin with good fundamentals whose tiny population has faded from the marketplace. Its price has more than doubled since the close of sales and the mint state Jackson brings almost as much as its rarer sibling, the Van Buren Seated Liberty. Interestingly enough neither one of these coins is even close to being the lowest mintage in the mint state First Spouse series, but they are displaying key and semi key price behavior anyway.

Modern gold collectors who want to collect scarce material by design instead of date, mintmark and finish only have a few options. They can acquire about 30 $5 gold commemoratives whose lead coins have become very expensive with key date mintages in the 5,000 to 8,000 range or they can put together a costly mint state $10 First Spouse set made up of about 40 half ounce gold coins with multiple key dates sporting mintages close to 3,000 coins. The only other option is to go with the short set concept that tends to show up when the cost of completion becomes a burden.

Unlike the three-coin $10 gold commemoratives that have an almost complete lack of thematic and design cohesion to hold them together, the Liberty gold subset has both Presidential and antique Liberty themes and designs that have distinguished them as a complete set and struck a chord with the collecting public.

Jackson's Capped Bust Liberty was struck as a member of the right set at the right time. The program's inaugural sales spike had collapsed and bulk buyers had lost interest thus setting the stage for the development we are seeing today.

2008-W PROOF $10
First Spouse Gold
Andrew Jackson's Liberty

OVERALL 3.5 SCORE

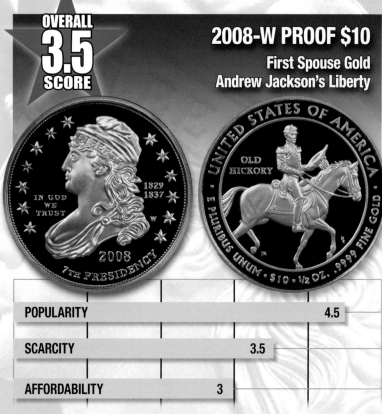

POPULARITY			4.5
SCARCITY		3.5	
AFFORDABILITY	3		

STATISTICAL INFORMATION

Mintage: 7,684

Obverse Designer: John Reich

Reverse Designer: Justin Kunz

Diameter: 26.49 mm

Weight: 15.554 grams

Composition: .9999 gold

AGW: .5 oz.

Edge Type: reeded

ESTIMATED RETAIL VALUE

UNCERTIFIED	NGC PF69 UC	NGC MS70 UC
$1,600	$1,650	$2,100

2008-W Proof $10 First Spouse Gold Andrew Jackson's Liberty

This beautiful gold issue was created because Andrew Jackson, the seventh president, did not serve with a wife. The obverse of the coin features a Capped Bust half dollar design that was issued from 1807 to 1836 with a lettered edge and was the coin of choice for silver deposits of the era.

The reverse shows Major General Jackson, affectionately known by his men as "Old Hickory," astride a horse. He willingly suffered his soldiers' hardships and was a hard willed leader. His victory at the Battle of New Orleans near the end of the War of 1812 was so one-sided he became the greatest national hero since George Washington, and it set him on a path that eventually lead to the Presidency.

The initial enthusiasm enjoyed by this series had largely abated by the time this coin was offered to collectors, but the beauty and historical significance of the proof Jackson Liberty was enough to make it the best selling First Spouse issue that year. By this point the market was already distinguishing between the generic First Spouse issues and the much more popular Liberty gold subset, both in initial sales numbers and after-market pricing.

This coin is not only desirable in the eyes of First Spouse series collectors. It's also desired by the budget conscious. Many collectors pass by the whole Spouse series because it requires the purchase of over $30,000 worth of gold. Instead, they buy only the four good looking coins that comprise the Liberty gold subset that can be purchased for less than $6,000.

Many collectors whose primary interest is in the "classics," show an interest in this particular issue because it's the only way to acquire a cameo proof Capped Bust half, even if it is struck on gold instead of silver.

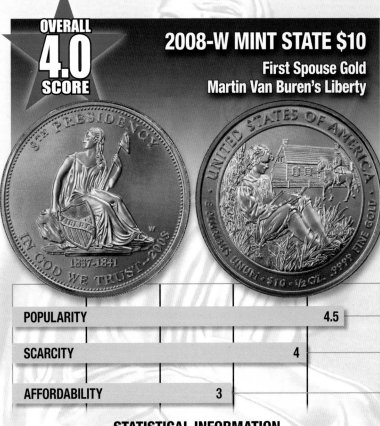

OVERALL 4.0 SCORE

2008-W MINT STATE $10
First Spouse Gold
Martin Van Buren's Liberty

POPULARITY				4.5
SCARCITY			4	
AFFORDABILITY		3		

STATISTICAL INFORMATION

Mintage: 3,826

Obverse Designer: Christian Gobrecht

Reverse Designer: Thomas Cleveland

Diameter: 26.49 mm

Weight: 15.554 grams

Composition: .9999 gold

AGW: .5 oz.

Edge Type: reeded

ESTIMATED RETAIL VALUE

UNCERTIFIED	NGC MS69	NGC MS70
$1,700	$1,750	$2,250

2008-W Mint State $10 First Spouse Gold Martin Van Buren's Liberty

This coin is the rarest of the four mint state and four proof coins in the Liberty gold subset. It was the eighth issue in the First Spouse gold program and the third Liberty issue.

It is typical for a series to go though an inaugural sales spike followed by a continuous deterioration in sales until the bottom is reached somewhere between the sixth and 10th issue, assuming material prices are close to stable.

This coin came along at the right time. Sales were still falling for the series, but the mint state Van Buren Seated Liberty looked like it was selling almost as well as the previous Jackson's Capped Bust Liberty.

At the end of the one-year sales period, the Mint's weekly sales report indicated that 4,461 had sold. In actuality there had been numerous order cancellations and returns that drove the mintage back down to 3,826. This was the lowest known mintage modern gold coin offered the pubic up to that time.

When the final audited number came out of the Mint, the after-market price of the coin doubled in a short period of time. The final Liberty issue, the Buchanan, came out less than two years later and sold relatively well, leaving this coin the mintage leader of the Liberty subset as seen below.

Mint State Liberty Gold Subset	Mintages
Jefferson's Draped Bust Liberty	19,823
Jackson's Capped Bust Liberty	4,609
Van Buren's Seated Liberty	3,826
Buchanan's Coronet Liberty	5,162

Rarity isn't everything. Good looking coins that are dominant in a series that is well liked tend to mature well. This coin is the undisputed king of the Liberty subset, has classic good looks that attracts both classic and modern collectors and is rarer than the well-respected proof 1936 Walking Liberty half.

2008-W PROOF $10

First Spouse Gold
Martin Van Buren's Liberty

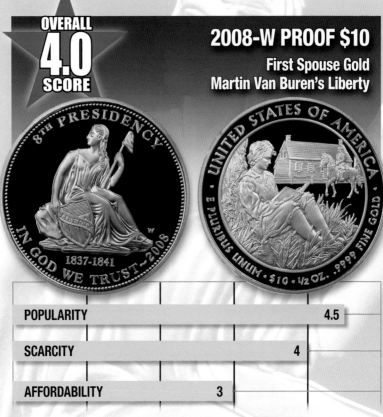

POPULARITY					4.5
SCARCITY				4	
AFFORDABILITY		3			

STATISTICAL INFORMATION

Mintage: 6,807

Obverse Designer: Christian Gobrecht

Reverse Designer: Thomas Cleveland

Diameter: 26.49 mm

Weight: 15.554 grams

Composition: .9999 gold

AGW: .5 oz.

Edge Type: reeded

ESTIMATED RETAIL VALUE

UNCERTIFIED	NGC PF69 UC	NGC PF70 UC
$1,600	$1,650	$2,100

2008-W Proof $10 First Spouse Gold Martin Van Buren's Liberty

The Van Buren's Liberty, or as it is sometimes referred to by those who collect the series as "Seated Liberty gold," was created because the eighth president's wife died when she was 35. Per the enabling legislation, presidents who did not serve with a spouse would use classic Liberty designs current during their tenure.

The obverse of the coin features the design that first appeared on the Liberty Seated dime between 1837 and 1891 as executed by Christian Gobrecht. "Sameness" and "unified designs" were the order of the day in the 1800s. Seated Liberty silver came in half dime, dime, 20-cent, quarter, half dollar and dollar form. It did not go out of service until 1891, so it was appropriate that the design have representation in the modern Liberty subset.

The reverse image shows a young Martin Van Buren at the tavern operated by his family in the town of Kinderhook, N.Y.

By the time this coin came out the series was in a slow and steady sales decline that continued for years. The sales reports from the Mint's Office of Public Affairs indicated that 7,515 coins had sold, but in fact after order cancellations and heavy use of the 30-day return option granted the buyers the final mintage was only 6,807 coins. This significant drop proved to be enough to make it the lowest mintage of the four proof coins in the Liberty subset, although it was far from obvious at the time that it would hold on to that distinction considering the overall mintage trends.

This coin isn't even close to being the rarest First Spouse gold issue, but it's priced like it is. That's because the proof coins in the Liberty gold subset are well liked by many. This coin's status as the key is now certain because the last of the Liberty subset, the Buchanan, finished out at 7,110 coins. The mintage chart of the four proof coins is listed below.

Proof Gold Liberty Subset	Mintages
Jefferson's Draped Bust Liberty	19,815
Jackson's Capped Bust Liberty	7,684
Van Buren's Seated Liberty	6,807
Buchanan's Coronet Liberty	7,110

2010-W MINT STATE $10
First Spouse Gold
James Buchanan's Liberty

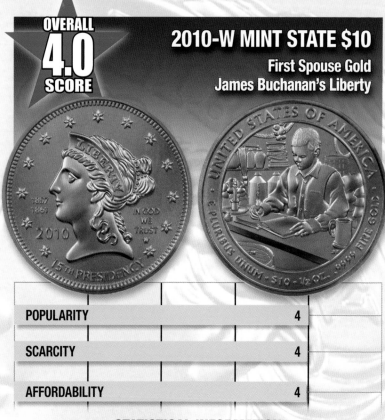

POPULARITY	4
SCARCITY	4
AFFORDABILITY	4

STATISTICAL INFORMATION

Mintage: 5,162

Obverse Designer: Christian Gobrecht

Reverse Designer: David Westwood

Diameter: 26.49 mm

Weight: 15.554 grams

Composition: .9999 gold

AGW: .5 oz.

Edge Type: reeded

ESTIMATED RETAIL VALUE

UNCERTIFIED	NGC MS69	NGC MS70
$1,000	$1,050	$1,275

2010-W Mint State $10 First Spouse Gold James Buchanan's Liberty

Two of the findings of the Citizens Coinage Advisory Committee's (CCAC) report to Congress regarding the late 1990s commemorative coin sales collapse were that the market can only absorb about two commemorative programs a year, and good designs with a classic look are readily absorbed while less attractive designs are not.

In many ways, the First Spouse series has the physical characteristics of a $10 gold commemorative program. Every design is different, each has its own theme and the series is a type set. That being the case, the CCAC statements suggesting that numerous high dollar issues that lack good looks produced over a relatively short period of time tend to get passed over by the public proved amazingly accurate.

The Liberty gold subset on the other hand, of which this coin is the last, fits the CCAC recommendations model for commemoratives beautifully. The four-coin Liberty subset is a short, affordable set of coins with classic good looks struck on gold. Buchanan's Coronet Liberty represented the closure of the four-coin Liberty gold subset, and it was a clear demonstration of strength.

Within weeks of going on sale the initial Mint inventory of 3,000 coins sold out. Almost immediately the Mint's marketing department announced that a second striking run was coming and it sold out well before the scheduled closing date. Sales were up 35 percent over the relatively rare Van Buren's Seated Liberty and finished out at 5,162 coins.

The coin's reverse showing Buchanan as a child in his father's print shop was selected as a default because Buchanan's presidency from a historian's perspective did not offer many viable themes or accomplishments of note. Thankfully the obverse suffered no such limitation.

The Coronet Head Liberty was the workhorse obverse design for U.S. gold on most denominations from the late 1830s until President Theodore Roosevelt came on the scene at the turn of the 20th century. If a collector desires a well struck and flawless example of this well-respected design in a mint state form, this Eagle-sized $10 gold coin is the only option.

2010-W PROOF $10
First Spouse Gold
James Buchanan's Liberty

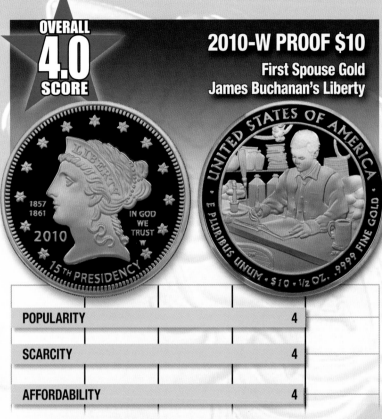

POPULARITY			4	
SCARCITY			4	
AFFORDABILITY			4	

STATISTICAL INFORMATION

Mintage: 7,110

Obverse Designer: Christian Gobrecht

Reverse Designer: David Westwood

Diameter: 26.49 mm

Weight: 15.554 grams

Composition: .9999 gold

AGW: .5 oz.

Edge Type: reeded

ESTIMATED RETAIL VALUE

UNCERTIFIED	NGC PF69 UC	NGC PF70 UC
$1,100	$1,150	$1,400

2010-W Proof $10 First Spouse Gold James Buchanan's Liberty

James Buchanan's Liberty was the fourth and final design in the popular Liberty gold subset that is part of the First Spouse series. The obverse selected for the coin features the image of Liberty wearing a coronet that was applied in various forms to almost every gold denomination struck by the federal government from the late 1830s until it was phased out of service starting in 1907. The well-respected design was executed by Christian Gobrecht.

Large denomination cameo proof Liberty head Gold Eagles are frequently referred to as the "Rolls Royce" of United States coinage. The $10 Liberty head proof Gold Eagles with and without "In God We Trust" on them have an estimated combined population of less than 2,000 coins after 69 years of production. They are large, lovely coins struck on about half an once of gold. They are rare and carry a $20,000 to $50,000 price tag. As a result, only very well financed collectors can acquire an example.

Buchanan's Liberty, like its terribly expensive proof ancestor, is a $10 federal issue struck on a half once of gold with a Liberty head for an obverse. The reverse image shows Buchanan as a child working in his father's print shop. It's the ONLY option if you like the look of high-grade antique proof gold but have to live within a reasonable budget.

With its 7,110 mintage it is only 4 percent more common than the rarest coin in the Liberty gold subset. If the public likes a coin, then a 7,110 mintage is plenty low enough to give it legs. A prime example of this is the over 100,000 mintage Ultra High Relief $20 Gold Eagles and the impressive price growth they have seen over the last few years.

This attractive $10 proof gold coin is the last issue of an affordable four-coin set that is in some ways a tour of the great designs of the 1800s that can't be acquired in a cameo proof format any other way. The popularity of the Liberty gold proofs is likely to continue to grow for all the right reasons.

OVERALL 4.0 SCORE

1995-W PROOF
10th Anniversary $1 Silver Eagle

POPULARITY					5
SCARCITY					5
AFFORDABILITY	2				

STATISTICAL INFORMATION

Mintage: 30,125

Obverse Designer: Adolf A. Weinman

Reverse Designer: John Mercanti

Diameter: 40.6 mm

Weight: 31.103 grams

Composition: .999 silver

ASW: 1.0 oz.

Edge Type: reeded

ESTIMATED RETAIL VALUE

UNCERTIFIED	NGC PF69 UC	NGC PF70 UC
$2,750	$3,100	$12,500

1995-W Proof
10th Anniversary $1 Silver Eagle

The 10th anniversary Silver Eagle is full of important lessons that all collectors need to master if they would like to see their collections mature well.

A 30,000 mintage proof issue is not "rare" compared to classic proofs issued prior to World War II or to most strong modern proofs for that matter. No, this coin is a textbook case of the importance of relative rarity in large population series.

Below is a mintage chart of all the cameo proof Silver Eagles, except for the reverse proofs of 2006 and 2011.

This coin is 12 times rarer than the next closest cameo proof issue, and some type of troubled infancy issue had to arise in order to create it. In the case of the 1995-W, the Mint offered a special 10th anniversary set that celebrated the commencement of Silver Eagle production at the West Point Mint. This coin was only available when purchased in a five-coin set that included four Gold Eagles.

The set became available rather late in the year when many people had already made their Eagle purchases. For some Silver Eagle collectors, it was an inconvenience to buy the set and sell the gold. To others it was nothing short of a hardship, but those with foresight who made the sacrifice were well rewarded for their effort.

There are many circumstances that create great series keys. It can be high initial purchase prices for large denominations, short sales and production periods, planchet shortages, too many competing offerings that spread collector dollars thin, collector indifference or any number of other considerations. But a wise collector watches for these anomalies and acts.

Great coins are not normally great in their own right just because they are rare. There are plenty of coins in the world that are rare but have little value. Coins are so often great in the context of the series over which they exercise dominance.

OVERALL 4.5 SCORE

2006-P REVERSE PROOF
20th Anniversary $1 Silver Eagle

POPULARITY				5
SCARCITY		3		
AFFORDABILITY				5

STATISTICAL INFORMATION

Mintage: 248,875

Obverse Designer: Adolph A. Weinman

Reverse Designer: John Mercanti

Diameter: 40.6 mm

Weight: 31.103 grams

Composition: .999 silver

ASW: 1.0 oz.

Edge Type: reeded

ESTIMATED RETAIL VALUE

UNCERTIFIED	NGC PF69	NGC PF70
$210	$240	$500

2006-P Reverse Proof
20th Anniversary $1 Silver Eagle

The proof Silver Eagle series is blessed with fantastic beauty.

James Baker, who was Secretary of the Treasury under President Reagan, felt that Adolph Weinman's iconic image on the Walking Liberty half was a fitting obverse for the new silver dollar. John Mercanti's soft and natural heraldic Eagle image was selected to complement the classic style of the obverse.

Proof Silver Eagles have been extremely well liked by the public from the beginning, and it shows up in the sales numbers year after year. One problem with this type of success is that it keeps the lower mintage dates common to the point that they don't develop prestige as they age.

Fortunately, the Mint has produced three relatively scarce anniversary issues, two of which are reverse proofs that complement the common dates and give the series numismatic flare that it would otherwise lack.

The Mint has been fairly consistent in offering reverse proofs for special occasions. As this series goes on we could very easily see the reverse proof Silver Eagles become a popular short set that modern silver dollar collectors focus on.

The 2006-P reverse proof Silver Eagle with its 248,875 mintage, while not the rarest reverse proof or proof Silver Eagle, is the first of its kind. As large and important to the modern collector as this series is, that's noteworthy in its own right.

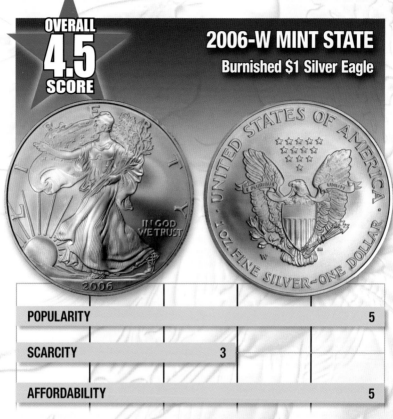

2006-W MINT STATE
Burnished $1 Silver Eagle

OVERALL 4.5 SCORE

POPULARITY					5
SCARCITY			3		
AFFORDABILITY					5

STATISTICAL INFORMATION

Mintage: 466,573

Obverse Designer: Adolph A. Weinman

Reverse Designer: John Mercanti

Diameter: 40.6 mm

Weight: 31.103 grams

Composition: .999 silver

ASW: 1.0 oz.

Edge Type: reeded

ESTIMATED RETAIL VALUE

UNCERTIFIED	NGC MS69	NGC MS70
$75	$100	$240

2006-W Mint State Burnished $1 Silver Eagle

The Silver Eagle series came into being for the same reason that the Morgan dollar was created by the Bland-Allison Act of 1878. America needed to use up huge amounts of silver for the benefit of domestic mines.

The Federal government had effectively been supporting the price of silver by building a National Defense Silver Stockpile that amounted to well over 100 million ounces by 1982. The Reagan administration at the time wished to see the material sold in bulk over a three-year period, but the effort was blocked by mining interests that claimed it would be financially disastrous to them and the people that they employed. After several failed attempts, a silver dollar capable of consuming huge quantities of silver from the National Defense Stockpile was added to the Liberty-Ellis Island Commemorative Coin Act and the Silver Eagle was born.

When the governmental objective in striking a coin is utilization of precious metal and not a need for coinage in common commerce, the mintage can grow almost without constraint, and the coins have a tendency to stay in high grade. Approximately 657 million Morgans were struck and even after the great melt of 1918, there were still 387 million of them in the hands of the public and government vaults. Every good-looking common date Morgan was a silent advertisement encouraging the public to start collecting the series. This series with inexpensive common dates went on to become a cornerstone of U.S. numismatics as the series matured.

The modern silver dollar is likely to become pivotal for the same reasons. At the current sales rate Silver Eagles will surpass the Morgan's surviving population in four years. Into the midst of this sea of coins the Mint has started issuing very low mintage mintmarked dollars that have tiny populations compared to their common date sibling, much like the Carson City dollars have tiny mintages compared to many other Morgans.

With its 466,573 mintage the 2006-W was the first low mintage mintmarked dollar to enter this series, setting the stage for what we see transpiring today – a huge set ruled by a handful of mintmarked dollars bound for eventual greatness.

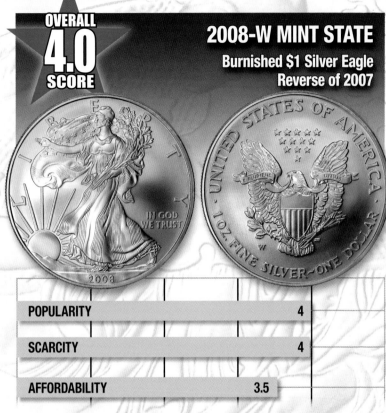

OVERALL
4.0
SCORE

2008-W MINT STATE
Burnished $1 Silver Eagle
Reverse of 2007

POPULARITY	4
SCARCITY	4
AFFORDABILITY	3.5

STATISTICAL INFORMATION

Mintage: Less than 46,318

Obverse Designer: Adolph A. Weinman

Reverse Designer: John Mercanti

Diameter: 40.6 mm

Weight: 31.103 grams

Composition: .999 silver

ASW: 1.0 oz.

Edge Type: reeded

ESTIMATED RETAIL VALUE

UNCERTIFIED	NGC MS69	NGC MS70
$440	$500	$775

2008-W Mint State Burnished
$1 Silver Eagle Reverse of 2007

For 2008, the Mint performed minor design revisions on the Silver Eagle reverse, but it used in-stock 2007 reverse dies to strike a few coins, giving this series its first major variety.

When the coins were first discovered the big question was, how many are there? In response, the West Point Mint checked its die strike records and determined that 16 of the 2007 reverse dies were used to strike 46,318 of the 2008-W Silver Eagles.

The report given to the public under a Freedom of Information Act request did not indicate that any effort was made to sort them out of inventory before they were shipped out to customers, but the coins still had to make it through quality control like everything else. The likelihood of making it from the coining press to the hands of the public was significantly less than 100 percent.

Below is the composite for most of the single-issue Eagles struck and shipped from 2006 to 2008. Notice that the very high scrap rate in 2008 creates a prospect of mintages much lower than the widely quoted 46,318 coins.

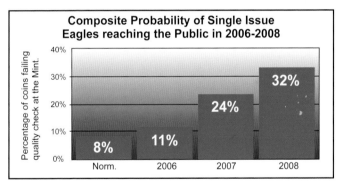

If collectors who are working on the series by date and mintmark come to the conclusion that they must have a 2008-W/07 to complete their set then it has a bright future. The 1995-W proof Silver Eagle has a similar mintage and a typical example is now valued at $3,000.

The Morgan dollar that in so many ways is this series' forerunner is actively collected by die variety known as VAMS. There is no reason to expect that the same tendency will not show up with this coin to some extent as it ages.

OVERALL
4.5
SCORE

2011-P REVERSE PROOF
25th Anniversary $1 Silver Eagle

POPULARITY				5
SCARCITY			4.5	
AFFORDABILITY		4		

STATISTICAL INFORMATION

Mintage: 100,000

Obverse Designer: Adolph A. Weinman

Reverse Designer: John Mercanti

Diameter: 40.6 mm

Weight: 31.103 grams

Composition: .999 silver

ASW: 1.0 oz.

Edge Type: reeded

ESTIMATED RETAIL VALUE

UNCERTIFIED	NGC PF69	NGC PF70
$325	$350	$675

2011-P Reverse Proof
25th Anniversary $1 Silver Eagle

The Mint occasionally makes glorious miscalculations in demand. Such is the story of the 2011-W reverse proof 25th anniversary $1 Silver Eagle.

Proof Silver Eagles have one of the largest collector followings of any modern series, so when a new special issue is planned the big question is, how many should be offered? In theory, the Mint wants to make just a bit fewer coins than it can sell so everyone who successfully places an order is grateful to receive it, there is no leftover inventory to be melted and relatively few customers are left out.

There are various models used to predict expected demand based on past sales behavior. The only problem is that none of it is better than an educated guess. If you look at weekly sales report behavior over the years for popular one-year issues, it's clear that 60 to 80 percent of the entire year's sales show up in the first four to six weeks. The Mint could have a one month open ordering period in the spring, strike to those sales numbers, ship in the fall and sell the few leftovers from problem orders in a small secondary offering late in the year. No backed up phone lines, no extra inventory, slightly tight supply, consistent after-market for the coins and no one to blame but yourself for not ordering one if you wanted one.

Until production is based on coin specific ordering data we will continue to have occasional miscalculations that produce five-hour sellouts as witnessed with the 25th anniversary silver set that included this coin.

Series need relatively scarce key dates among their members to give them numismatic flare and create interest. The 1995-W cameo proof was another mistake/opportunity that priced the typical Silver Eagle buyer out of the market. The 100,000 mintage seen on the 2011-P reverse proof makes the perfect crown jewel for the typical Silver Eagle collector. It's rare enough to provide pride of ownership but it does not cost $3,000.

The 2011 25th anniversary reverse proof was both a glorious gift to the series and the kind of anomaly that moderns collectors with foresight look for. Below is the mintage profile of the proof Silver Eagle series.

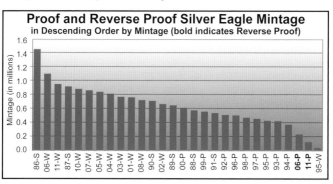

OVERALL 4.5 SCORE

2011-S MINT STATE
25th Anniversary $1 Silver Eagle

POPULARITY				5
SCARCITY				4.5
AFFORDABILITY			3.5	

STATISTICAL INFORMATION

Mintage: 100,000

Obverse Designer: Adolph A. Weinman

Reverse Designer: John Mercanti

Diameter: 40.6 mm

Weight: 31.103 grams

Composition: .999 silver

ASW: 1.0 oz.

Edge Type: reeded

ESTIMATED RETAIL VALUE

UNCERTIFIED	NGC MS69	NGC MS70
$300	$340	$495

2011-S Mint State
25th Anniversary $1 Silver Eagle

If you believe that rarity is relative then this coin is of great interest. In Silver Eagle sets collected strictly by date and mintmark this coin has no peer. It is about 4.6 times rarer than the next lowest mintage "W" issues, shown below in red, and 36 times rarer than the scarcest bulk issued coin shown in blue.

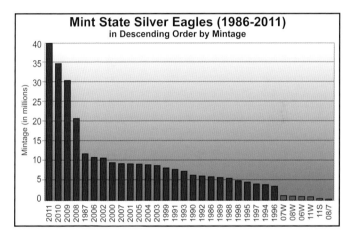

The 2011-S is the first non-commemorative "S" mintmarked high silver content dollar struck since the 1935-S Peace dollar. Silver Eagles are the largest precious metal series seen in almost 50 years and have a strong collector following to go with them. So when the 25th anniversary set was announced the market recognized the coin for what it was and forced a 100,000 set sellout in five hours.

A rational question is will the 2011-S with its 100,000 mintage prove rare enough to hold onto lead coin status, and if so, will it appreciate?

In regard to appreciation, there are 2,800 common dates out in the hands of the public for every 2011-S. Even the mighty 1995-W proof Silver Eagle that we covered previously has only about 600 common dates pushing on it for every key date that exits and that is enough to give it a current market price of about $3,000.

OVERALL 4.0 SCORE

1999-W MINT STATE
Struck With Unfinished Proof Dies
$5 Gold Eagle

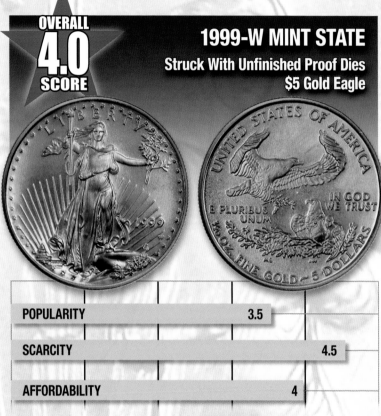

POPULARITY	3.5
SCARCITY	4.5
AFFORDABILITY	4

STATISTICAL INFORMATION

Mintage: (6,000)

Obverse Designer: Augustus Saint-Gaudens

Reverse Designer: Miley Busiek

Diameter: 16.6 mm

Weight: 3.393 grams

Composition: .9167 gold, .03 silver, .0533 copper

AGW: .10 oz.

Edge Type: reeded

ESTIMATED RETAIL VALUE

UNCERTIFIED	NGC MS69	NGC MS70
$700	$900	$4,000

1999-W Mint State Struck With Unfinished Proof Dies $5 Gold Eagle

The 1999-W mint state $5 Gold Eagle is one of modern numismatic's great mysteries. It's a coin that's not supposed to exist, much like the 1913 Liberty head nickel is not supposed to exist.

U.S. Mint history is full of examples of non-sanctioned special coins that made it into the hands of the public and whose long-term destiny was numismatic greatness. The 1999-W mint state $5 Gold Eagle may prove to be just such a coin.

In 1999, in the midst of the Y2K gold buying panic, West Point Mint production exploded forcing lax quality control. Whether intentional or unintentional, unpolished proof dies were used to strike a few "W" mintmarked issues. These coins were discovered in early 2000 to the amazement of the numismatic community.

Hundreds of these coins were found, including pure rolls. One of the earliest researchers on this topic was Fred Weinberg, who was able to determine that some of the large initial recipients of $5 and $10 1999-W gold were jewelry fabricators in Asia. As a result, many of these scarce coins met an immediate unfortunate fate.

After persistent inquiry's into the likely production numbers associated with mint state 1999-W gold, the U.S. Mint's Office of Public Affairs stated in 2005 that dies for the $5 mint state gold coins were changed on average after every 6,000 coins were minted.

Twelve years after being struck, the two primary grading services have received a total of about 5,000 1999-W mint state $5 Gold Eagles to be graded. These numbers are deceiving, however, because many graded examples have been cracked out of their holders and sent back though multiple times in hopes of higher grades. Today, fresh, never-graded material is not coming to market in the frequency or volume that it used to.

Coins go on to greatness not just because they are good looking or rare. Most of the time they need to be the rarest coin in a large popular series that is collected in such a manner that there is no way around needing that coin to achieve completion. The 1999-W mint state $5 Gold Eagle for years was a lone mintmarked coin in a set that was collected predominately by date. Some called the coin an "error" because of the uncertainty associated with its creation.

The coming of the 2006-W, 2007-W and 2008-W fractional gold changed the way modern Eagle collectors put together their sets. They are not just date sets anymore. Complete Gold Eagle sets are collected by date and mintmark.

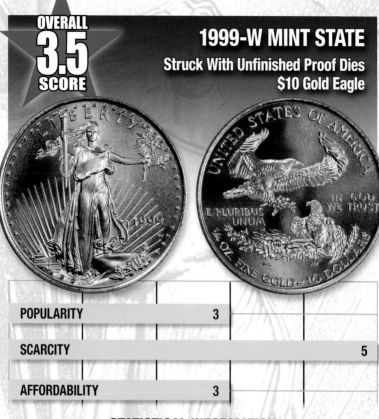

OVERALL 3.5 SCORE

1999-W MINT STATE
Struck With Unfinished Proof Dies
$10 Gold Eagle

POPULARITY		3		
SCARCITY				5
AFFORDABILITY		3		

STATISTICAL INFORMATION

Mintage: (6,000)

Obverse Designer: Augustus Saint-Gaudens

Reverse Designer: Miley Busiek

Diameter: 22.0 mm

Weight: 8.48 grams

Composition: .9167 gold, .03 silver, .0533 copper

AGW: .25 oz.

Edge Type: reeded

ESTIMATED RETAIL VALUE

UNCERTIFIED	NGC MS69	NGC MS70
$1,300	$1,600	$14,000

1999-W Mint State Struck With Unfinished Proof Dies $10 Gold Eagle

There are certain coins in each collecting generation that need to be acquired in high grade early on because over time the few that exist find long-term homes, and the price they command once they have had time to mature can "lock you out." Such seems to be the case for the 1999-W mint state $10 Gold Eagle.

The mint state $10 Gold Eagle series that these coins inhabit have a lot going for them. They are large enough to see well without magnification, millions of good looking relatively affordable common dates are already in the hands of the public, and the dominant coins in this series look like they could end up rarer than the established keys in the other Gold Eagle denominations.

Of the currently existing "W" mintmarked Gold Eagles, only the 1999-W was struck and shipped in bulk. All the other "W" mintmarked Gold Eagles were individually struck, handled, and packaged so they are easy to acquire in very high grade. This is not the case with the 1999-W. Most have handling blemishes to some extent, and it's hard to find the kind of perfection present in the 2006-W, 2007-W and 2008-W Gold Eagles.

Like its 1999-W mint state $5 gold sibling, we have very few answers as to why this coin exists. We do know that the Y2K explosion of demand for gold probably contributed to its creation and 12 years after their release the two primary grading services have received a total of 3,000 1999-W mint state $10 Gold Eagles to be graded. But it is likely that many of those coins were cracked out of their holders and sent back many times to be regraded in hopes of receiving a higher grade.

Unless something changes and more 1999-W $10 gold coins are found per year over the next 10 years than were found in the first 12 years, then this coin in high grade could end up without peer since FDR recalled personal gold in 1933.

For years the 1999-W was a mintmark rarity in sets that were collected by date, but now it's obvious to the causal observer that all the low mintage modern Eagles, be they silver, gold or platinum, are mintmarked special issues. Mintmarked modern Eagles are the dominant coins in the most extensive large denomination series issued since the Great Depression, and collectors with foresight are actively acquiring an example of each now.

OVERALL 3.0 SCORE

2006-W REVERSE PROOF
20th Anniversary $50 Gold Eagle

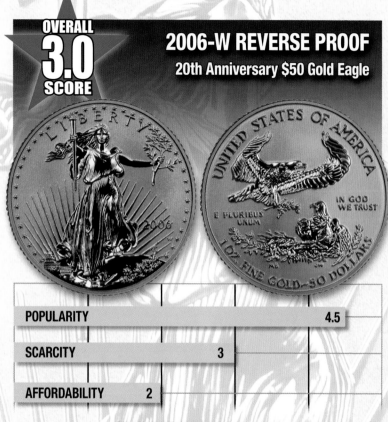

POPULARITY				4.5
SCARCITY		3		
AFFORDABILITY	2			

STATISTICAL INFORMATION

Mintage: 9,996

Obverse Designer: Augustus Saint-Gaudens

Reverse Designer: Miley Busiek

Diameter: 32.7 mm

Weight: 33.93 grams

Composition: .9167 gold, .03 silver, .0533 copper

AGW: 1.0 oz.

Edge Type: reeded

ESTIMATED RETAIL VALUE

UNCERTIFIED	NGC PF69	NGC PF70
$2,500	$2,650	$3,500

2006-W Reverse Proof 20th Anniversary $50 Gold Eagle

This coin, with its 9,996 mintage, is by far the lowest mintage modern proof Gold Eagle ever struck regardless of denomination. From the day that it was offered to the public in the 20th anniversary set it has enjoyed exceptional collector interest.

It is the only reverse proof Gold Eagle issued thus far in a series that is over 25 years old. Given that the Mint allowed the silver anniversary of the series to pass without creating another one, it's likely to remain the only $50 reverse proof gold issues for the foreseeable future.

Completing the $50 Gold Eagle set is a daunting task financially for the typical collector because regardless of whether you pursue a $50 set in mint state or proof form, you must purchase over 25 ounces of gold in addition to the key dates. The 20th anniversary three-coin gold set with the reverse proof, cameo proof and uncirculated issue represented one of every type of $50 gold finish in an attractive package. The 20th anniversary gold set is a natural type set that serves as an affordable alternative to collecting the whole series.

Not only do collectors of the entire $50 proof gold set and type set collectors want the 20th anniversary reverse proof, so do anniversary set collectors. Below is a list of all the anniversary Eagle sets that have been issued thus far, along with their mintages.

Anniversary Set	Mintage
10th anniversary 5-coin Silver and Gold Eagle set	30,102
20th anniversary 3-coin Gold Eagle set	9,996
20th anniversary 3-coin Silver Eagle set	248,875
10th anniversary 2-coin Platinum Eagle set	16,937
25th anniversary 5-coin Silver Eagle set	100,000

Notice that this very beautiful coin is a triple key. It's the rarest $50 proof Gold Eagle, the rarest Gold Eagle type coin and the rarest modern anniversary issue. What a marvelous convergence!

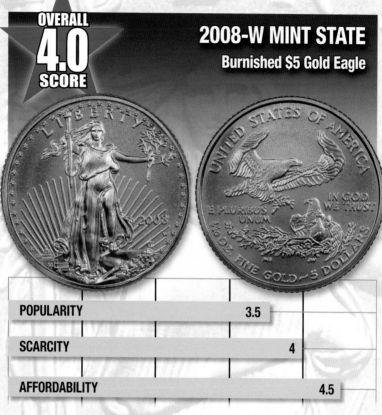

OVERALL 4.0 SCORE

2008-W MINT STATE
Burnished $5 Gold Eagle

POPULARITY	3.5	
SCARCITY	4	
AFFORDABILITY		4.5

STATISTICAL INFORMATION

Mintage: 12,657

Obverse Designer: Augustus Saint-Gaudens

Reverse Designer: Miley Busiek

Diameter: 16.5 mm

Weight: 3.393 grams

Composition: .9167 gold, .03 silver, .0533 copper

AGW: .10 oz.

Edge Type: reeded

ESTIMATED RETAIL VALUE

UNCERTIFIED	NGC MS69	NGC MS70
$300	$315	$450

2008-W Mint State
Burnished $5 Gold Eagle

The $5 Gold Eagle sets are the most affordable and easiest to complete of all U.S. gold coin series. When you consider that the quarter Eagle Indian series is the closest antique equivalent and costs about $35,000 for a MS-63 set, the $5,000 to $6,000 complete set price for $5 Gold Eagles graded MS-69 is attractive.

Huge numbers of good looking common dates in the hands of the public serve as silent advertising for the series. This set's 12 million population has already exceeded that of the similar sized classic quarter Eagle gold Indians. The U.S. Mint gave this set a much needed gift when it struck a series of four "W" mintmarked Gold Eagles with mintages at least seven times rarer than the next closest non-mintmarked issue.

The 2008-W should not be scarce or rare relative to the other mintmarked issues. The Mint allocated 27,461 raw planchets for 2008-W $5 uncirculated Gold Eagle production, which should have been enough for everyone who wanted one that year, but that's not how it turned out. Fifty-four percent of them were scrapped and only 12,657 made it out the door, leaving a gaping hole in the mintage tables that we see today. This coin is 20 times rarer than its typical quarter of a million mintage siblings. Nothing but the $5 1999-W is capable of challenging this coin for supremacy in its set.

If you look back over coinage history for the last 100 years or so there is a clear tendency for smaller denomination coinage to have a higher appreciation rate as it matures than larger denominations assuming they are struck on the same metal. For the patient, good things really do come in small packages, and that is certainly true of key date fractional gold if it's purchased before it matures.

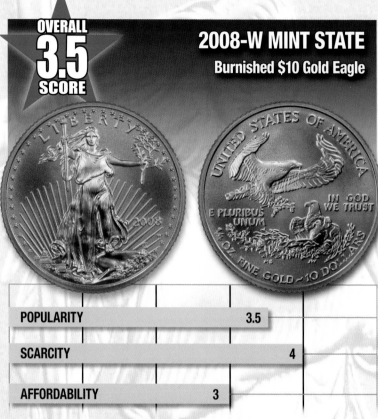

OVERALL 3.5 SCORE

2008-W MINT STATE
Burnished $10 Gold Eagle

POPULARITY	3.5	
SCARCITY		4
AFFORDABILITY	3	

STATISTICAL INFORMATION

Mintage: 8,883

Obverse Designer: Augustus Saint-Gaudens

Reverse Designer: Miley Busiek

Diameter: 22.0 mm

Weight: 8.48 grams

Composition: .9167 gold, .03 silver, .0533 copper

AGW: .25 oz.

Edge Type: reeded

ESTIMATED RETAIL VALUE

UNCERTIFIED	NGC MS69	NGC MS70
$1,500	$1,550	$1,750

2008-W Mint State Burnished $10 Gold Eagle

Every few years a convergence of events presents collectors with a true gift coin. The 2008-W mint state burnished $10 Gold Eagle is just such an issue. Not only does it posses a modern rendition of Augustus Saint-Gaudens' highly regarded Double Eagle on the obverse and an attractive "Family of Eagles" design on the reverse, it has an 8,883 mintage to go with it.

American collectors have a long history of collecting series by date and mintmark, and starting in 2006 the Mint decided that it would issue uncirculated mintmarked gold for sale directly to the public instead of through its authorized dealer network. This split collector demand between mintmarked and non-mintmarked coins and drove the sales numbers down.

On top of this the Mint is required by law to strike bulk Gold Eagles "in quantities sufficient to meet public demand." The problem was that public demand for gold in 2008 was nothing short of staggering, and the Mint had precious little extra planchet capacity or time for what were considered secondary programs.

Only 16,332 planchets were struck and a horrific scrap rate of 46 percent gave us a final mintage of 8,883. Within months of the close of sales, the Mint issued a statement that it was eliminating all fractional "W" mintmarked gold from the annual product offerings. Thus, this worthy anomaly was created by a very fortunate convergence of events.

Well over 3 million of these attractive and affordable fractional Gold Eagles are now in the hands of the public. There are very few U.S. gold series that offer collectors of average means any hope of assembling a complete, high grade set of coins for just over the price of the metal they are stuck on. In the midst of this set stand two coins that rule it with an iron hand. This is one of them.

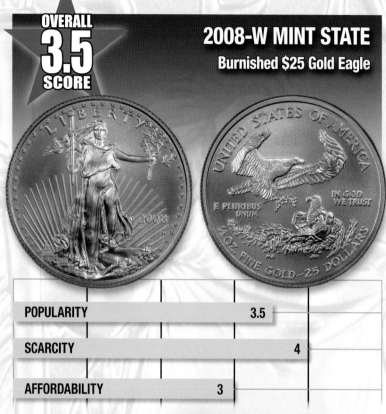

OVERALL 3.5 SCORE

2008-W MINT STATE
Burnished $25 Gold Eagle

POPULARITY	3.5	
SCARCITY		4
AFFORDABILITY	3	

STATISTICAL INFORMATION

Mintage: 15,683

Obverse Designer: Augustus Saint-Gaudens

Reverse Designer: Miley Busiek

Diameter: 27.0 mm

Weight: 16.96 grams

Composition: .9167 gold, .03 silver, .0533 copper

AGW: .50 oz.

Edge Type: reeded

ESTIMATED RETAIL VALUE

UNCERTIFIED	NGC MS69	NGC MS70
$1,500	$1,550	$1,750

2008-W Mint State Burnished $25 Gold Eagle

The mint state $25 Gold Eagle has the lowest average mintage of all four denominations of the mint state Gold Eagles series. This has attracted the attention of many collectors and dealers.

For years their primary focus was the 1986 to 1991 halves with Roman numerals known as Type 1 modern gold. High-grade examples of the 1991 half with its 24,100 mintage were widely considered the strongest coin in the denominational set. As the years rolled on it looked like it was going to endure as the uncontested series key. That all changed with the Mint's decision to produce "W" mintmarked fractional gold starting in 2006.

The 2006-W was struck to anticipated demand and sold out at 15,164 coins, eclipsing the previously low mintage 1991 half by 9,000 coins. In 2007, although 19,698 planchets were allocated to the coin, an abnormally high scrap rate brought the final mintage down even further to 11,455.

Thanks to the offering of a two-coin set called the "Double Prosperity Set" that offered a 2008-W mint state $25 Gold Eagle and gold Buffalo, the final mintage of the 2008-W gold half moved back up to 15,683. In any case, the three "W" mintmarked Gold Eagles are very well liked and are serious contenders for dominance in their set.

While the 2008-W may not be as rare as the 2007-W, it is fortunate to enjoy a halo effect from the general mintage crash that appeared in 2008, along with the termination of the "W" mintmarked fractional gold offering in 2009.

The $25 Gold Eagles are a very attractive set to collectors because they are large enough to be physically impressive, but you don't have to spend the kind of money it takes to put together the 1 ounce set.

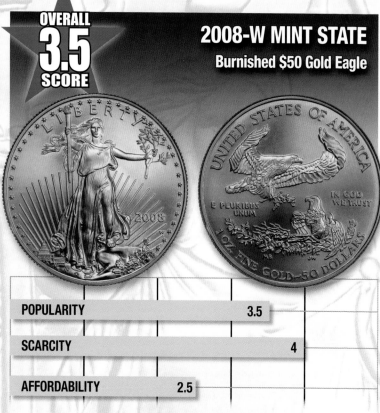

OVERALL 3.5 SCORE

2008-W MINT STATE
Burnished $50 Gold Eagle

POPULARITY	3.5	
SCARCITY		4
AFFORDABILITY	2.5	

STATISTICAL INFORMATION

Mintage: 11,908

Obverse Designer: Augustus Saint-Gaudens

Reverse Designer: Miley Busiek

Diameter: 32.7 mm

Weight: 33.93 grams

Composition: .9167 gold, .03 silver, .0533 copper

AGW: 1.0 oz.

Edge Type: reeded

ESTIMATED RETAIL VALUE

UNCERTIFIED	NGC MS69	NGC MS70
$2,100	$2,150	$2,400

2008-W Mint State Burnished $50 Gold Eagle

The gold bullion act of 1985 that created this coin stated that the obverse was to be a depiction of Liberty and the reverse design was to portray a family of Eagles with the male bringing an olive branch back to the nest. The administration at the time felt that there was no finer depiction of Liberty than the one created by Augustus Saint-Gaudens for the double Eagle, so then Secretary of the Treasury James Baker instructed that a slender version of Saint-Gaudens' Liberty be used.

The image of Liberty striding forth out of the rising sun, standing on the rock, holding a torch and olive branch symbolizing light and peace has no doubt contributed to this coin's stunning success. Additionally, they are acceptable for inclusion in various federally sanctioned retirement programs. In total over 15 million $50 Gold Eagles have been purchased by the public through the authorized dealer network.

Starting in 2006, the Mint began offering mintmarked versions of this coin directly to the public. In the third year of the "W" mintmarked issues the Mint experienced a debilitating spike in demand for Gold Eagles and per the legislation that created this series the Mint was obligated to strike the non-mintmarked issues in "volumes sufficient to meet public demand," leaving very few planchets or time for the non-essential "W" mintmarked programs. Although 18,909 2008-W $50 coins were struck, only 11,908 of them made it past quality control and into the hands of the public. These coins were caught in the mintage crash of 2008.

For those who like to own good looking gold for just over melt this series is a wonderful option. The 2008-W $50 Gold Eagle is approximately 35 times rarer than the typical Gold Eagle, and it adds numismatic potential and flare to an otherwise very common series.

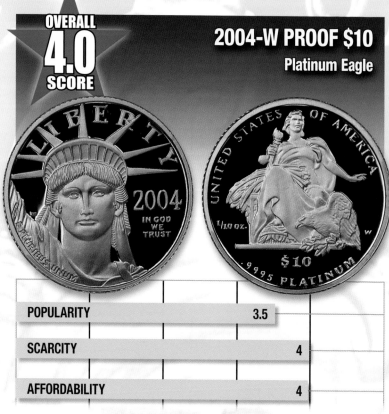

OVERALL 4.0 SCORE

2004-W PROOF $10
Platinum Eagle

POPULARITY			3.5	
SCARCITY			4	
AFFORDABILITY			4	

STATISTICAL INFORMATION

Mintage: 7,161

Obverse Designer: John Mercanti

Reverse Designer: Donna Weaver

Diameter: 16.5 mm

Weight: 3.112 grams

Composition: .9995 platinum

APW: .10 oz.

Edge Type: reeded

ESTIMATED RETAIL VALUE

UNCERTIFIED	NGC PF69 UC	NGC PF70 UC
$475	$500	$750

2004-W Proof $10 Platinum Eagle

The enabling legislation for proof Platinum Eagle coins gives no design or thematic guidance thus allowing the Mint a free hand in selecting great designs and themes every year without congressional input.

Proof Platinum Eagles were the first U.S. coins to enjoy the Mint's revolutionary stable obverse and annually changing reverse structure that later became popularized by the 50 States quarter program.

For 2004 the proof platinum reverse theme was to be "America – the Land of Plenty." Donna Weaver modeled her seated design on Daniel Chester French's Depiction of America, which is one of the four statues outside the New York Customs house known as the "Continents."

In 1899 the United States Department of the Treasury contracted Cass Gilbert to design and build a customs house that showed the greatness and grandeur of the United States. In 1903 he asked Daniel Chester French and August Saint-Gaudens to submit designs for the sculptures, but Saint-Gaudens declined the request due to his workload.

It's a good thing because the "Continents," including America, were not finished and installed until 1907. Those same closing years of Saint-Gaudens' life gave us the Saint-Gaudens Double Eagle and the $10 Indian. Little did Daniel Chester French know that he, too, was creating great coinage art. It was just going to take 100 years to show up with some help from Donna Weaver.

Like many of the great allegorical images of the early 1900s, a beautiful robed woman carrying a burning torch of enlightenment with her right hand represents the emergence of hope and liberty for the people of the Americas. Seated America has her right foot on the head of Quetzalcoatl, the old plumed serpent deity of Central and South American cultures, while across her lap are full stalks of corn representing the bounty that true enlightenment surely brings. A bald Eagle is resting at her feet.

The 2004 $10 America Seated proof, along with its 2008 judicial reverse sibling, are the strongest coins in their 12-member set, and unlike the 2008 issue Seated America, only came in proof form. Historic artwork, a 7,161 mintage and reasonable cost make for a fine combination.

OVERALL 3.5 SCORE

2004-W PROOF
$25 Platinum Eagle

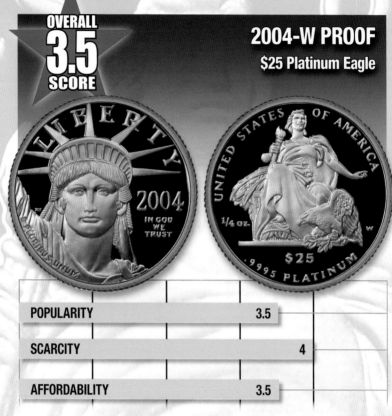

POPULARITY	3.5
SCARCITY	4
AFFORDABILITY	3.5

STATISTICAL INFORMATION

Mintage: 5,193

Obverse Designer: John Mercanti

Reverse Designer: Donna Weaver

Diameter: 22.0 mm

Weight: 7.78 grams

Composition: .9995 platinum

APW: .25 oz.

Edge Type: reeded

ESTIMATED RETAIL VALUE

UNCERTIFIED	NGC PF69 UC	NGC PF70 UC
$1,000	$1,050	$1,500

2004-W Proof
$25 Platinum Eagle

It's important for collectors to pick up on changes in the way sets are being put together while it's happening.

A good example of this took place from about 1890 to 1920 when collectors were moving from collecting by date run to collecting by date and mintmark. Those who did not make the adjustment early on missed out on fantastic opportunities.

Since the late 1990s the Mint has consistently offered large changing reverse series to the public in the form of 50 States and National Parks quarters, Presidential dollars, Native American dollars and to a lesser degree the Life of Lincoln cents and Westward Journey nickels.

Many collectors develop their habits putting together sets with pocket change, so it's reasonable to assume that over time high-end series that have this structure will do very well. This is where the Platinum Eagles come in. They are the only changing reverse high-end set with designs that are consistently good. And for now, the set only costs about 50 percent more than the value of the metal they are struck on.

The 2004 Seated America proof $25 Platinum Eagle in particular is the creation of an interesting convergence of circumstances. The Platinum Eagles were experiencing the typical downward drift in sales that new series frequently go through. Then, to make things worse, the price of platinum forced the prices on new issues up about 50 percent from 2002 to 2004. Very few collectors and almost no speculators showed up to purchase them. When the market realized only 5,193 of them made it out the Mint's door, the hunt for them was on. The 2004 Seated reverse was the first Platinum Eagle to carry a substantial premium.

We know from watching the behavior of old series that smaller denominations out perform the larger ones if the coins all have the same design and are struck on the same metal. This being the case, the $25 issue struck on a quarter ounce of platinum is a nice balance between being affordable and large enough to see the design without magnification.

The 2004 Seated America and the 2008 Legislative proof Platinum Eagles clearly dominate their series, but the Seated America has the distinction of being offered only in proof form.

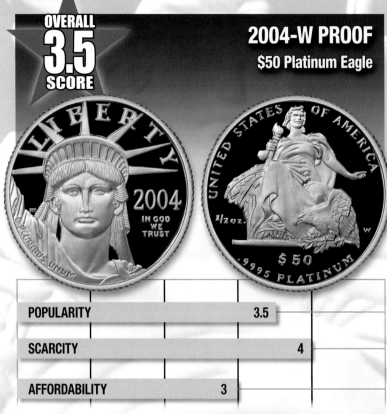

OVERALL 3.5 SCORE

2004-W PROOF
$50 Platinum Eagle

POPULARITY		3.5	
SCARCITY			4
AFFORDABILITY	3		

STATISTICAL INFORMATION

Mintage: 5,063

Obverse Designer: John Mercanti

Reverse Designer: Donna Weaver

Diameter: 27.0 mm

Weight: 15.56 grams

Composition: .9995 platinum

APW: .50 oz.

Edge Type: reeded

ESTIMATED RETAIL VALUE

UNCERTIFIED	NGC PF69 UC	NGC PF70 UC
$1,600	$1,650	$2,200

2004-W Proof
$50 Platinum Eagle

Proof Platinum Eagle halves, as they are called, are an impressive 13-coin set. Its members are all good looking and have a mintage listing that looks like the seven-coin mintage table on proof Walking Liberty halves struck prior to World War II.

But unlike the Walking Liberty halves, these coin have the up and coming changing reverse "collector series" structure, as the Mint likes to call it. And they are struck on a half-ounce of platinum instead of about half an ounce of silver. The proof platinum halves, unlike the proof Walkers, are not likely to get hurt if the next generation of collectors decides to emphasize design change in their sets.

The 2004 proof Platinum Eagles in particular were released for sale mid-year and had seen a 50 percent price increase since the 2002 coin. To make matters worse, in 2005 the Mint tried to offer coins earlier in the year for customers who had special occasions during the first half of the year. This produced a short sales year for the 2004 and left the Mint with significant unsold inventory that was ultimately disposed of. Until the mintage crash of 2008, the 2004 proof platinum half was the poster child for low mintage modern design-based type coins and had a price that reflected that fact.

Even though the 2008 "Legislative" half with its 4,020 mintage has eclipsed the 2004 Seated America issue's rarity, the 2004 still commands about the same price in the market place. This can be attributed to either the four-year head start the 2004 had in finding long-term homes or superior popularity of the design. In any case, it's unusual for a modern coin that was eclipsed in a series mintage chart to hold on so well for so long.

Like many other noteworthy fractional Eagle programs, the Mint stopped making proof platinum halves after 2008 in order to concentrate demand on the $100 proof issues.

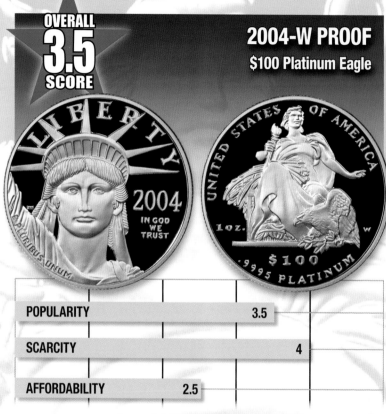

2004-W PROOF
$100 Platinum Eagle

POPULARITY	3.5	
SCARCITY		4
AFFORDABILITY	2.5	

STATISTICAL INFORMATION

Mintage: 6,007

Obverse Designer: John Mercanti

Reverse Designer: Donna Weaver

Diameter: 32.7 mm

Weight: 31.12 grams

Composition: .9995 platinum

APW: 1.0 oz.

Edge Type: reeded

ESTIMATED RETAIL VALUE

UNCERTIFIED	NGC PF69 UC	NGC PF70 UC
$2,200	$2,300	$3,600

2004-W Proof
$100 Platinum Eagle

The U.S. Mint says the proof $100 Platinum Eagle is its "premiere offering."

It is the longest running changing reverse collector series, despite the fact that it didn't quite make the sales benchmark in 2008.

Starting with the 2009 dated coins, the Mint issued a statement that it wanted to only offer those coins that the public buys often. That meant that programs that are not required by law that don't sell 10,000 or so coins will not survive. Given that the 2008 proof $100 Platinum Eagle only sold 4,796 coins, it's interesting that the Mint chose to continue the program.

U.S. Mint Director Ed Moy stated at the Artistic Infusion Symposium in 2008 that "we have unlimited design opportunities with our 24–karat gold and platinum coins. Let us not waste those opportunities."

In short, this series is one of the few blank canvases given to the Mint by Congress, and it is not in a hurry to part with it.

In 2009, the fractional proof Platinum Eagles and all mint state platinum issues were suspended thus concentrating all Platinum Eagle demand on the $100 proof denomination. At the same time the Mint kicked off a new multi-year subset based on the Preamble to the Constitution. Sales on these coins were in the 8,000 to 15,000 range and the series survived.

If coin collecting is the hobby of kings then the proof $100 Platinum Eagle set is an excellent candidate for their interest. The coins are large, with well-executed designs, low mintages, the highest U.S. denomination, and struck on the rarest of coinage metals.

The 2004 in many ways epitomizes what is right with this series. Not only is its 6,007 mintage extremely low for a 1 ounce coin, its Seated America design inspired by the work of Daniel Chester French, a contemporary of Augustus Saint-Gaudens, has a magnetism that affords it a special status in modern platinum collections.

This young set, including its key dates of 2004 and 2008, trades at close to the cost of the material they are struck on, so if you want to own platinum, this is a beautiful and cohesive way to do it.

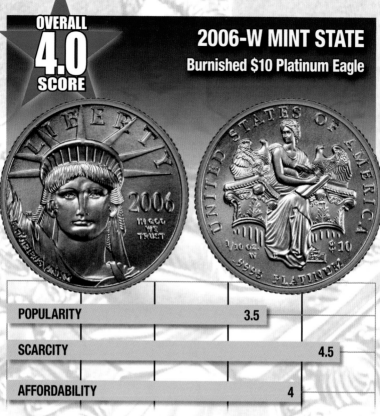

OVERALL
4.0
SCORE

2006-W MINT STATE
Burnished $10 Platinum Eagle

POPULARITY			3.5	
SCARCITY				4.5
AFFORDABILITY			4	

STATISTICAL INFORMATION

Mintage: 3,544

Obverse Designer: John Mercanti

Reverse Designer: Joel Iskowitz

Diameter: 16.5 mm

Weight: 3.112 grams

Composition: .9995 platinum

APW: .10 oz.

Edge Type: reeded

ESTIMATED RETAIL VALUE

UNCERTIFIED	NGC MS69	NGC MS70
$400	$415	$550

2006-W Mint State
Burnished $10 Platinum Eagle

The 2006-W $10 mint state Platinum Eagle is the rarest dime-sized type coin (specific design, denomination and finish) to be issued to the public since the $2.5 matte proof Indian Gold Eagle was produced from 1908 to 1915. Initial public interest in matte proof Indians was tepid, and production was eventually suspended as a result, but today they trade at over $10,000 each.

Almost exactly 100 years later, the Mint faced the same situation. The $10 mint state Platinum Eagles are no longer offered because they did not sell well, and the planchet shortage that started in 2008 did not leave any capacity for coins that were not required by Congress.

There have been a total of five types of $10 business issue/mint state Platinum Eagles since the program was introduced in 1997. The first seven years of production had a reverse proof finish much like the reverse proof anniversary coins that we see today. It was expensive to polish reverse proof dies by hand prior to automation of the process, so a matte finish was employed starting in 2004 and continued until the series was suspended in 2008. Inadvertently, the Mint saved the best for last.

The three-year theme for the "W" mintmarked Platinum Eagles for 2006, 2007 and 2008 was the "Foundations of American Democracy." These were the three years that the mint state Platinum Eagles received the same changing reverse designs as their proof counterparts and created a mintage anomaly. The total mintages based on type are listed below.

Reverse Design	Mintage
1997 to 2003 Eagle over the Sun – Reverse Proof Appearance	296,786
2004 to 2008 Eagle over the Sun – Matte Finish	70,027
2006-W Legislative	3,544
2007-W Executive	5,556
2008-W Judicial	3,706

A type set of these coins is very affordable, and the last three issues – of which the 2006-W is king – are amazingly rare.

U.S. coinage history is full of "sleeper" coins with good fundamentals that were initially overlooked by the public and later went on to become truly great. The similarly sized matte proof Indians are a fitting example of what small, rare overlooked coins are capable of doing when they finally take off.

2006-W MINT STATE
Burnished $25 Platinum Eagle

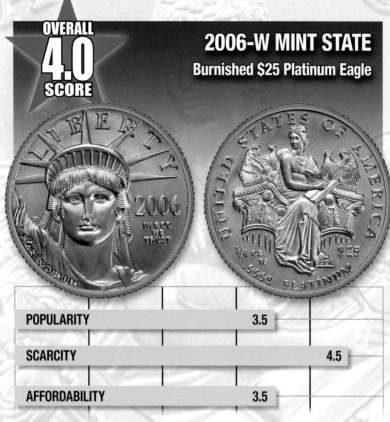

POPULARITY		3.5	
SCARCITY			4.5
AFFORDABILITY		3.5	

STATISTICAL INFORMATION

Mintage: 2,676

Obverse Designer: John Mercanti

Reverse Designer: Joel Iskowitz

Diameter: 22.0 mm

Weight: 7.78 grams

Composition: .9995 platinum

APW: .25 oz.

Edge Type: reeded

ESTIMATED RETAIL VALUE

UNCERTIFIED	NGC MS69	NGC MS70
$600	$625	$850

2006-W Mint State
Burnished $25 Platinum Eagle

One of the things that Mint management values about the Platinum Eagle series is the complete thematic and design freedom that it has in producing the coins thanks to the very generous language of the enabling legislation.

After pressing a runner-up design from 2004 into service in 2005, Mint management felt that if it was going to keep the coin it was time for a new multi-year theme. The three-year Foundations of American Democracy concept commemorating the three branches of our governmental system was chosen. Coins would be struck in the order in which the branches of government were developed in the Constitution.

Joel Iskowitz designed the 2006 reverse called the "Legislative Muse" based on the marble statue known as "The Car of History," one of the original statues in the Old Hall of the House of Representatives. Iskowitz replaced the winged Chariot of Time accompanying the Muse with a pair of Corinthian columns representing the two houses of Congress. The coin gave platinum collectors one more good design for their set.

The mint state $25 Platinum Eagle set took on outstanding rarity and design differentiation like the 50 State quarters with the introduction of the 2006-W "Legislative quarter," as platinum collectors often refer to it.

Almost without exception, the 1/10th ounce and 1 ounce coins sell the best to the general public leaving the 1/4 ounce and 1/2 ounce issues the low mintage option. This was the case in 2006, yielding a final mintage of 2,676, an almost unheard of number.

This fantastically rare type sets members are large enough to enjoy without magnification, have high material content as a percentage of their purchase price, and are relatively affordable. The mint state/business strike type set listings are shown below.

$25 Business Strike Platinum Type Set	Mintage
1997-2003 Reverse Proof Appearance – Eagle Over the Sun	200,202
2004 –2008 Mint State – Eagle Over the Sun	73,226
2006-W Mint State – Legislative	2,676
2007-W Mint State – Presidential	3,690
2008-W Mint State – Judicial	2,481

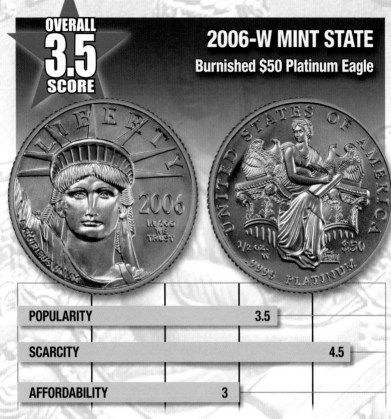

OVERALL
3.5
SCORE

2006-W MINT STATE
Burnished $50 Platinum Eagle

POPULARITY	3.5	
SCARCITY		4.5
AFFORDABILITY	3	

STATISTICAL INFORMATION

Mintage: 2,577

Obverse Designer: John Mercanti

Reverse Designer: Joel Iskowitz

Diameter: 27.0 mm

Weight: 15.56 grams

Composition: .9995 platinum

APW: .50 oz.

Edge Type: reeded

ESTIMATED RETAIL VALUE

UNCERTIFIED	NGC MS69	NGC MS70
$1,000	$1,050	$1,400

2006-W Mint State
Burnished $50 Platinum Eagle

A three-year run of mintmarked special issues for platinum, gold, and silver that was destined to deliver mintage anomalies in their sets began in 2006.

The $50 Platinum Eagles went on sale late in 2006 and to the shock of the collecting community, the little $10 coin went on backorder almost immediately, indicating that the whole set was short struck.

Ultimately 2,577 of the "Legislative halves," as collectors called them, were sold. The coin reigned as the king of modern design and denomination based rarity for a while and might still be king today if the mintage crash of 2008 hadn't created the Judicial reverse platinum super coins.

Platinum halves are a closed set due to the sweeping reduction of Mint offerings that took place in early 2009, so the collector does not face an open ended financial commitment while completing a set. The half dollar sized coins are large enough to be impressive, but don't contain anything like the amount of platinum seen in the larger and more numerous $100 coins.

Platinum Eagles are normally collected by type and not date. The shortest and most affordable type set is the mint state coins. The $50 proof and mint state type set is shown below.

Matte Finish Issues	**Mintage**
2006-W Mint State – Legislative	2,577
2007-W Mint State – Presidential	3,635
2008-W Mint State – Judicial	2,253
2004 –2008 Mint State "Bullion" – Eagle Over the Sun	52,852

Reverse Proof Appearance

1997-2003 Reverse Proof Bullion – Eagle Over the Sun	158,349
2007 Reverse Proof "Anniversary" – Presidential	16,873

Cameo Proofs

1997 Cameo Proof – Eagle Over the Sun	15,431
1998 Cameo Proof –New England Coast	13,836
1999 Cameo Proof – Wetlands	11,103
2000 Cameo Proof – Heartland	11,049
2001 Cameo Proof – Southwest	8,254
2002 Cameo Proof – Northwest	8,772
2003 Cameo Proof – Patriotic Vigilance	7,131
2004 Cameo Proof – Seated America	5,063
2005 Cameo Proof – Plenty	5,942
2006 Cameo Proof – Legislative	7,649
2007 Cameo Proof – Presidential	22,873
2008 Cameo Proof – Judicial	4,020

2006-W MINT STATE
Burnished $100 Platinum Eagle

POPULARITY		3.5	
SCARCITY			4
AFFORDABILITY	2.5		

STATISTICAL INFORMATION

Mintage: 3,068

Obverse Designer: John Mercanti

Reverse Designer: Joel Iskowitz

Diameter: 32.7 mm

Weight: 31.12 grams

Composition: .9995 platinum

APW: 1.0 oz.

Edge Type: reeded

ESTIMATED RETAIL VALUE

UNCERTIFIED	NGC MS69	NGC MS70
$2,100	$2,150	$2,500

2006-W Mint State
Burnished $100 Platinum Eagle

This double Eagle sized mint state coin is the largest denomination ever produced by the U.S. Mint, but it did not survive the offerings purge of early 2009 because its enabling legislation states that the series is optional. Just like the fractional mint state platinum issues, the $100 platinum type set is composed of five members, three of which are the rare Foundations of American Democracy coins.

Many collect Platinum Eagles by design in both proof and mint state form. The $100 proof Platinum Eagles are the only surviving platinum issue. Its current Preamble to the Constitution theme is scheduled through 2014, so the total expenditure is open ended and the set is large.

The $100 denomination is the only one that carries all the designs present in the Platinum Eagle type set. All demand for new Platinum Eagles is now forced to show up in the changing reverse $100 denomination. The Mint's marketing efforts for platinum are concentrated on the $100 proof coins, which are selling fairly well for a coin in their price range.

This type set is a silver dollar-sized collection that is the ultimate expression of the modern changing reverse (like 50 States quarters) structure. The complete $100 combined proof and mint state type set mintages are listed below.

1997 Proof – Eagle Over the Sun 20,851
1998 Proof – New England 14,912
1999 Proof – Wetlands 12,363
2000 Proof – Heartland 12,453
2001 Proof – Southwest 8,969
2002 Proof – Northwest 9,834
2003 Proof – Patriotic Vigilance 8,246
2004 Proof – Seated America 6,007
2005 Proof – Plenty 6,602
2006 Proof – Legislative 9,152
2007 Proof – Executive 8,363
2008 Proof – Judicial 4,769
2009 Proof – Perfect Union 7,945
2010 Proof – Establish Justice 9,871
2011 Proof – Tranquility 15,000

1997 to 2003 Reverse Proof Appearance – Eagle Over the Sun ... 289,291
2004 to 2008 Mint State – Eagle Over the Sun 48,321

2006-W Mint State – Legislative 3,068
2007-W Mint State – Executive 4,177
2008-W Mint State – Judicial 2,876

OVERALL 3.5 SCORE

2007-W REVERSE PROOF
10th Anniversary $50 Platinum Eagle

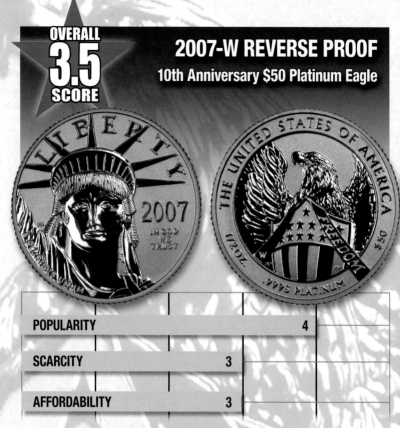

POPULARITY			4
SCARCITY		3	
AFFORDABILITY		3	

STATISTICAL INFORMATION

Mintage: 16,937

Obverse Designer: John Mercanti

Reverse Designer: Tom Cleveland

Diameter: 27.0 mm

Weight: 15.56 grams

Composition: .9995 platinum

APW: 0.50 oz.

Edge Type: reeded

ESTIMATED RETAIL VALUE

UNCERTIFIED	NGC PF69	NGC PF70
$950	$1,050	$1,400

2007-W Reverse Proof
10th Anniversary $50 Platinum Eagle

In 2007, the Mint wanted to offer a 10th anniversary Platinum Eagle to follow on the heels of the extremely successful 20th anniversary gold and silver sets issued in 2006. But which denomination or denominations should be chosen, and how many should be offered?

The primary 20th anniversary silver and gold sets were composed of three 1 ounce Eagles: a cameo proof, a reverse proof and a "W" mintmarked issue. The sets were very impressive and well received, but if the same scenario was used for the 10th anniversary platinum set the cost would have been between $4,000 and $5,000, well beyond the reach of many collectors.

In order to create a 10th anniversary platinum set with coins large enough to be impressive, while still remaining affordable, a pair of Presidential reverse $50 Platinum Eagles were chosen. The two-coin set consisted of a common cameo proof and a reverse proof that was exclusive to the set.

The Mint struck 30,000 platinum sets representing three times the number of gold anniversary sets sold the previous year. Ultimately, 16,937 10th anniversary platinum sets ended up in the hands of the public; the rest were melted.

The 10th anniversary set is a gift to the $50 proof Platinum Eagle series because reverse proof anniversary type collectors want the $50 gold, $50 platinum and $1 reverse proof Silver Eagles for their collection.

This coin floating around in the hands of the public is a great way to get then started collecting the $50 proof Platinum Eagle series. It's a great introduction to a lovely changing reverse set.

It's interesting to note that the inaugural $50 bullion issue Platinum Eagle that came out in 1997 also had a reverse proof appearance, but the raised surfaces chosen for polish were not the same. On the 10th anniversary issue, Liberty had a highly reflective face and neck, while the early reverse proofs had a reflective crown, robe and hair with a matte finish face. The 1997 inaugural reverse proof is pictured along with the 10th anniversary presidential version and its cameo proof anniversary set sibling.

2008-W MINT STATE
Burnished $10 Platinum Eagle

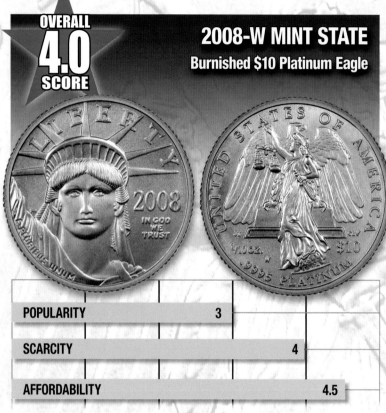

POPULARITY	3		
SCARCITY		4	
AFFORDABILITY			4.5

STATISTICAL INFORMATION

Mintage: 3,706

Obverse Designer: John Mercanti

Reverse Designer: Joel Iskowitz

Diameter: 16.5 mm

Weight: 3.112 grams

Composition: .9995 platinum

APW: 0.10 oz.

Edge Type: reeded

ESTIMATED RETAIL VALUE

UNCERTIFIED	NGC MS69	NGC MS70
$300	$315	$450

2008-W Mint State Burnished $10 Platinum Eagle

If you collect business strike/mint state Platinum Eagles by type, and most people with an interest in the series do, then you only need five coins: two Eagle Over the Sun reverse issues, one being a reverse proof appearance bullion issue and the other being a matte finish, plus the three-coin Foundations of American Democracy issues.

These short little sets are struck on 1/10th ounce of platinum, can be completed in high grade for under $1,500 and are rarer than Mercury dime proof sets.

The structure of collector's sets tends to be influenced by what is being produced by the Mint, but there is a lag time before it shows up. The concept of the short set is not new to numismatics, but the current Mint practice of having thematic short sets with cohesive designs and changing reverses is.

New collectors being exposed to interesting thematic short sets like the Life of Lincoln cents, Westward Journey nickels and Sacagawea Native American reverse dollars are likely to gravitate to higher-end expressions of this structure as they mature. Mint employees have the tendency to call stable obverse changing reverse thematic sets "collector series."

The problem with most collector series is the key dates (rarest members) are so common that their long-term development prospects are limited. But being too common is not an issue when the entire population of the 2008-W or 2006-W $10 Platinum Eagles will fit in a lunch bag.

If you take the time to graph price growth rates verses denominations for various classic "unified design" issues that were prevalent in the 1800s and early 1900s, you will find that in general smaller denominations tend to grow in value faster than the large coins. Affordable series tend to pick up collector followings much more readily than larger denominations, and we can expect similar behavior for the very affordable and rare $10 Platinum Eagle.

The 2008-W $10 mint state Platinum Eagle and Foundations of American Democracy short set members are an interesting combination of rarity, affordability and design cohesion with a collector series reverse.

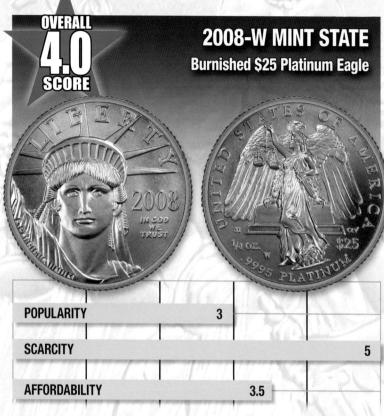

2008-W MINT STATE
Burnished $25 Platinum Eagle

POPULARITY	3	
SCARCITY		5
AFFORDABILITY	3.5	

STATISTICAL INFORMATION

Mintage: 2,481

Obverse Designer: John Mercanti

Reverse Designer: Joel Iskowitz

Diameter: 22.0 mm

Weight: 7.78 grams

Composition: .9995 platinum

AGW: 0.25 oz.

Edge Type: reeded

ESTIMATED RETAIL VALUE

UNCERTIFIED	NGC MS69	NGC MS70
$650	$675	$1,100

2008-W Mint State
Burnished $25 Platinum Eagle

Opportunity so often is found in overlooked places that have low risk and good long-term fundamentals. One such example may be the 2008-W mint state burnished $25 Platinum Eagle with the Judicial design reverse.

The West Point Mint struck 4,476 of the coins and of that number only 2,481 made it past quality control and into the hands of the public yielding a horrific 45 percent net scrap rate. If that wasn't bad enough, the Mint continued to take orders for coins it did not have in stock to protect itself from the possibility of returns, giving the misleading impression that these coins were relatively common.

Many speculators who bought hundreds of these coins looking at the rising price of platinum and bad mintage data felt the best thing to do was sell them to bullion houses to grab a profit. To reduce shipping costs, hundreds of them were mailed loose in boxes and plastic storage bags thus reducing the high-grade population even further. Talk about a promising convergence of troubled infancy issues for this particular issue.

Most platinum collectors put together sets based on profound differences in physical appearance. The $25 Platinum Eagle type set has five members. Their initial mintages are shown below.

Reverse Design	Mintage
1997 to 2003 Eagle over Sun – Reverse Proof Appearance ...	200,202
2004 to 2008 Eagle over Sun – Matte Finish	73,226
2006-W Legislative design	2,676
2007-W Executive design	3,690
2008-W Judicial design...	2,481

The $25 Foundations of American Democracy short set issues have mintage figures that are anomalies, yet the coins are affordable and physically large enough to enjoy without magnification.

Acquiring young U.S. type coins that have not gone through the growth phase of their life cycle yet with total populations in the low 2,000s are an opportunity that has not presented itself for at least three generations. If you look though David Bowers' *Guide Book of U.S. Type Coins* and take the average of his surviving population estimates, the 2008-W $25 Platinum Eagle places in the top 25 rarest type coins in the last 200 years.

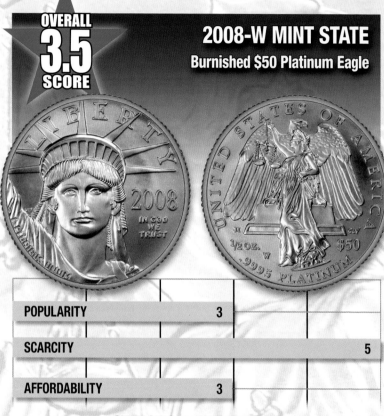

OVERALL
3.5
SCORE

2008-W MINT STATE
Burnished $50 Platinum Eagle

POPULARITY			3		
SCARCITY					5
AFFORDABILITY			3		

STATISTICAL INFORMATION

Mintage: 2,253

Obverse Designer: John Mercanti

Reverse Designer: Joel Iskowitz

Diameter: 27.0 mm

Weight: 15.56 grams

Composition: .9995 platinum

APW: 0.50 oz.

Edge Type: reeded

ESTIMATED RETAIL VALUE

UNCERTIFIED	NGC MS69	NGC MS70
$1,200	$1,250	$2,000

2008-W Mint State
Burnished $50 Platinum Eagle

This coin is the most profound design-based rarity offered to the public by the Federal government in mint state or proof since 1915.

Although 4,066 of them were struck, like many of the coins caught in the mintage crash of 2008, only 2,253 of them made it into the hands of the public resulting in an almost 50 percent scrap rate.

There were many more orders taken than there were coins to distribute, giving the market the impression that the coins were common when they were in fact exceptionally rare. Audited final numbers showing the 2,253 mintage did not come out for over a year after the close of sales.

As platinum's price moved past the coin's $635 purchase price in early 2009, some misinformed speculators holding more than they needed sold them off as common bullion.

The "Legislative Branch" reverse on the 2008-W $50 Platinum Eagle is the third design in the Foundations of American Democracy short set celebrating the three branches of American government. Initially, the designs were to be the Car of History from the chambers of Congress, the Presidential Seal, and an eagle and owl perched together symbolizing wisdom and power to represent the Judicial Branch. When the coin came out a blindfolded image of Justice dressed in a long gown holding scales in her right hand and a sword in the left with a great bald eagle at her back was the selection. Impressive or not, the collectors who were following the series were shocked.

The five-coin $50 mint state type set members are shown below.

Reverse Design	Mintage
1997 to 2003 Eagle over Sun – Reverse Proof Appearance.	158,349
2004 to 2008 Eagle over Sun – Matte Finish	52,852
2006-W Legislative design	2,577
2007-W Executive design	3,635
2008-W Judicial design	2,253

OVERALL
3.5
SCORE

2008-W MINT STATE
Burnished $100 Platinum Eagle

POPULARITY	3			
SCARCITY			4.5	
AFFORDABILITY	2.5			

STATISTICAL INFORMATION

Mintage: 2,876

Obverse Designer: John Mercanti

Reverse Designer: Joel Iskowitz

Diameter: 32.7 mm

Weight: 31.12 grams

Composition: .9995 platinum

APW: 1.0 oz.

Edge Type: reeded

ESTIMATED RETAIL VALUE

UNCERTIFIED	NGC MS69	NGC MS70
$2,100	$2,150	$3,000

2008-W Mint State
Burnished $100 Platinum Eagle

This coin is the rarest 1 ounce type coin issued to the general public by the U.S. Mint since the matte proof Saint-Gaudens Double Eagle was discontinued in 1915. Like its fractional siblings, it is the child of the 2008 mintage crash.

The Mint struck 5,084 coins, but only 2,876 were deemed of high enough quality to be sold to the public.

For most of our coinage history, the Mint had a policy of limited design change and "sameness" across denominations. Thirty- to 60-year production runs with basically the same design were common. Even with very low survival rates and in many cases low annual mintages, the surviving mint state type populations of most coins in the last 200 years are frequently higher than 3,000 coins, according to estimates of classic coin scholars such as Q. David Bowers.

While short production cycles don't ensure a design will achieve significant type rarity, it certainly does help, and a high scrap rate on top of very few coins struck is a beautiful thing. This $100 coin is so blessed.

The main thing holding this Judicial reverse Eagle and its series back in both proof and mint state form is that it's struck on platinum instead of gold, and the high material content of the series makes it costly to pursue. Only well financed collectors with an eye for that which is rare and out of the ordinary consider pursuing these coins, but those who do find them one of the most physically impressive and interesting collections offered in the last 100 years.

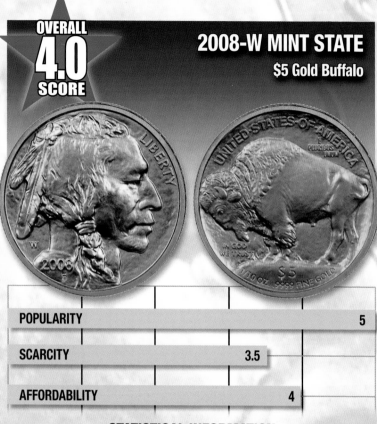

2008-W MINT STATE
$5 Gold Buffalo

POPULARITY					5
SCARCITY			3.5		
AFFORDABILITY			4		

STATISTICAL INFORMATION

Mintage: 17,429

Obverse Designer: James Earle Fraser

Reverse Designer: James Earle Fraser

Diameter: 16.5 mm

Weight: 3.11 grams

Composition: .9999 gold

AGW: 0.10 oz.

Edge Type: reeded

ESTIMATED RETAIL VALUE

UNCERTIFIED	NGC MS69	NGC MS70
$525	$550	$700

2008-W Mint State
$5 Gold Buffalo

The modern Buffalo issues have a direct lineage to the "golden era" of great artistic excellence that began with Theodore Roosevelt's dissatisfaction with U.S. coinage design and Augustus Staint-Gaudens' influence.

By 1911 the cent, $2.5, $5, $10 and $20 gold issues had already gone through impressive facelifts. The nickel was the only current production coin whose design was open to revision do to the 25-year design stability law of 1890. The Taft administration and his Secretary of the Treasury Franklin MacVeagh recognized the opportunity to "beautify the nickel" during their administration thus creating a "permanent souvenir of the most attractive sorts."

To this end, a public search for a new design began. James Earl Fraser, who became Augustus Saint-Gaudens' assistant after winning a competition that Saint-Gaudens had judged, applied for the job. He stated in a 1947 radio interview that "when I was asked to do the nickel, I felt I wanted to do something totally American – a coin that could not be mistaken for an other country's coin. It occurred to me the Buffalo as part of our western background was 100 percent American and that our North American Indian fitted into that picture perfectly."

Really great work ages well and that is certainly the case with the four new Buffalo denominations. The architects of the gold Buffalo enabling legislation required that .9999 fine gold coins be struck and that the reverse and obverse bear the 1913 Type 1 Buffalo designs by Fraser. Fractional coins were made optional and the Secretary of the Treasury could change the design after the first year, but the .9999 fine gold's design has run unmodified for almost a decade. That's a powerful endorsement of the gold Buffalo's popularity.

If the mint ever chooses to strike fractional mint state gold Buffalos regularly to complement the fractional Gold Eagles in the bullion program, the 2008-W $5 issue would likely become an immediate and strong key.

Currently, the 2008-W $5 gold Buffalo is the most common mint state fractional issue with its 17,429 mintage, but its classic good looks, long-term potential and affordable price makes it a collector favorite.

OVERALL 4.0 SCORE

2008-W MINT STATE
$10 Gold Buffalo

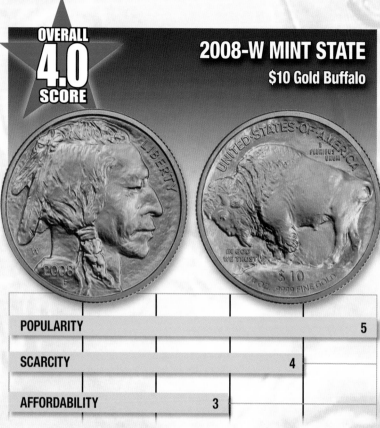

POPULARITY				5
SCARCITY			4	
AFFORDABILITY		3		

STATISTICAL INFORMATION

Mintage: 9,949

Obverse Designer: James Earle Fraser

Reverse Designer: James Earle Fraser

Diameter: 22.0 mm

Weight: 7.776 grams

Composition: .9999 gold

AGW: 0.25 oz.

Edge Type: reeded

ESTIMATED RETAIL VALUE

UNCERTIFIED	NGC MS69	NGC MS70
$1,250	$1,275	$1,550

2008-W Mint State $10 Gold Buffalo

This coin should be quite common for a modern fractional gold issue but as it is so often said, timing is everything.

The mint issued fractional Buffalo gold right before their bloated offering list was paired back dramatically in 2009 leaving this a one-year-only issue for the foreseeable future. On top of that, the West Point Mint struck 26,797 of these coins in 2008 and then proceeded to scrap 63 percent of them due to planchet, capacity and quality issues. Only 9,949 made it into the hands of collectors.

Below is a listing of the total number of modern mint state Buffalo issues for each denomination. As you can see, for modern Buffalo type collectors there is no contest in terms of which coin is king.

2001-D Mint State $1 Silver Buffalo 227,131
2006-2011 Mint State $50 Gold Buffalo..............................1,000,000+
2008-W Mint State $25 Gold Buffalo...16,908
2008-W Mint State $10 Gold Buffalo...9,949
2008-W Mint State $5 Gold Buffalo...17,429

The $10 fractional gold Buffalos are exceptionally popular with the public because they look like just like gold Buffalo nickels. The design and size is practically identical to the Buffalo nickel, except for the coin's denomination and purity inscriptions.

The Buffalo nickel is a well-respected classic series with a large and devoted following. The convergence of Buffalo nickel series collectors and modern type collectors on this coin gives it broad appeal.

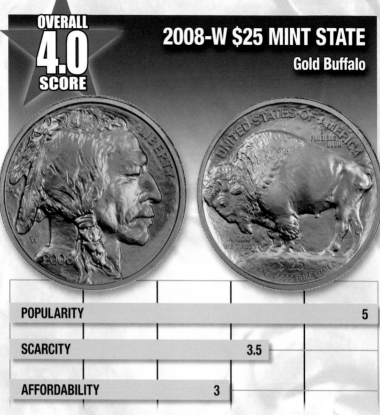

2008-W $25 MINT STATE
Gold Buffalo

OVERALL 4.0 SCORE

POPULARITY	5
SCARCITY	3.5
AFFORDABILITY	3

STATISTICAL INFORMATION

Mintage: 16,908

Obverse Designer: James Earle Fraser

Reverse Designer: James Earle Fraser

Diameter: 26.5 mm

Weight: 15.552 grams

Composition: .9999 gold

AGW: 0.50 oz.

Edge Type: reeded

ESTIMATED RETAIL VALUE

UNCERTIFIED	NGC MS69	NGC MS70
$1,200	$1,225	$1,550

2008-W $25 Mint State Gold Buffalo

This single year issue is one of the most common fractional gold Buffalos. Unlike its siblings, it was issued in a four-coin set, single issue and an unusual special issue called the Double Prosperity Set.

The Double Prosperity Set was an effort by the U.S. Mint to increase its market share and penetration into Asian markets. Eight is traditionally associated with prosperity in Asian cultures and the date 8-8-08 afforded special significance. To capitalize on this a two-coin set made up of a $25 uncirculated gold Buffalo and a $25 uncirculated Gold Eagle were marketed together in an attractive hardwood box. Ultimately, 7,622 Double Prosperity Sets were sold driving the 2008-W $25 uncirculated gold Buffalos mintage up to 16,908 coins.

Modern collectors like this coin for the same reason the Mint selected this denomination for the prosperity set. The $25 Buffalo is large enough to be physically impressive, enjoys classic good looks complements of Fraser's Buffalo nickel and is still affordable.

Prototype packaging for the Double Prosperity Set.

2008-W MINT STATE
$50 Gold Buffalo

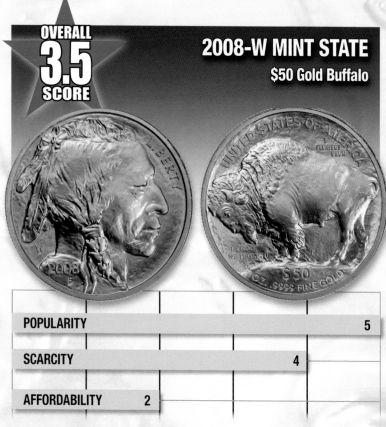

POPULARITY				5
SCARCITY			4	
AFFORDABILITY	2			

STATISTICAL INFORMATION

Mintage: 9,074

Obverse Designer: James Earle Fraser

Reverse Designer: James Earle Fraser

Diameter: 32.7 mm

Weight: 31.103 grams

Composition: .9999 gold

AGW: 1.0 oz.

Edge Type: reeded

ESTIMATED RETAIL VALUE

UNCERTIFIED	NGC MS69	NGC MS70
$2,800	$2,900	$3,600

2008-W Mint State $50 Gold Buffalo

Modern mint state Buffalo collectors tend to collect in one of two ways. They normally put together a 2008-W four-coin gold set and add the mint state Buffalo dollar to it thus becoming a type collector or they collect the $50 mint state issues in series by date and mintmark. In both cases the $50 2008-W is required for completion, and it's the rarest issue in the set.

The convergence of events that created the 2008 special issue mintage crash were especially pronounced for this coin. The West Point Mint's raw planchet supply and free capacity were stretched over too many issues. Although 21,374 planchets were struck, 58 percent of them did not make it past quality control and out the door into the hands of the public. Thus, only 9,074 coins exist.

Look at the gaping hole this coin creates in the series mintage chart below.

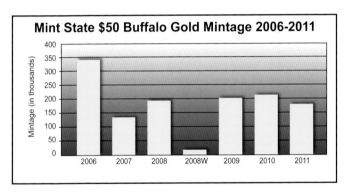

Now let's look at the typical type set mintage profile for the five-coin mint state set composed of the following issues:

Issue	Mintage
2001-D Mint State $1 Gold Buffalo	227,131
2008-W Mint State $5 Gold Buffalo	17,429
2008-W Mint State $10 Gold Buffalo	9,949
2008-W Mint State $25 Gold Buffalo	16,908
2008-W Mint State $50 Gold Buffalo	9,074

We don't know for a fact that the 2008-W $50 gold Buffalo will endure until the end of the series as the rarest of all, but it certainly looks likely. Serious modern Buffalo collectors are fully aware of this coin's dominance in their sets and try to pick one up if they can. It is the rarest of all proof and mint state issues.

2008-W PROOF
$5 Gold Buffalo

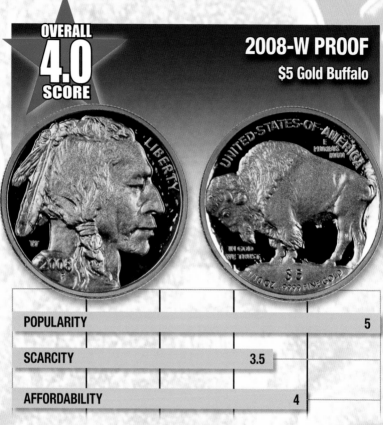

POPULARITY					5
SCARCITY			3.5		
AFFORDABILITY			4		

STATISTICAL INFORMATION

Mintage: 18,884

Obverse Designer: James Earle Fraser

Reverse Designer: James Earle Fraser

Diameter: 16.5 mm

Weight: 3.11 grams

Composition: .9999 gold

AGW: .10 oz.

Edge Type: reeded

ESTIMATED RETAIL VALUE

UNCERTIFIED	NGC PF69 UC	NGC PF70 UC
$650	$675	$825

2008-W Proof
$5 Gold Buffalo

The public has a long-standing tendency to favor proof special issues over their uncirculated counterparts, and it shows up in the mintage totals. The problem with this initial popularity is it normally translates into mintages that are so high that the proof coin lacks the scarcity it needs to mature well.

This particular proof issue enjoys proof popularity without a significantly higher mintage than the 2008 $5 uncirculated Buffalo because the Mint happened to strike them in roughly equal numbers before selling out late in 2008. Ultimately, 18,884 proof $5 gold Buffalos made it into the hands of the public out of the 24,725 stuck.

The benefits of superior collector demand without the typical increase in initial mintages has caused the proof $5 Buffalo to trade at values that are consistently higher than its $5 uncirculated sibling.

These coins were not required by Congress and were eliminated in the offering purge of early 2009 when fractional coinage that was not required by law was eliminated. This coin is currently a one-year-only type coin and as such is very special. The one wild card that this coin and the other fractional Buffalos face is the prospect of the return of fractional gold Buffalos to the Mint's offerings listing.

Buffalo gold is immensely popular and the Mint's marketing department is aware if this. The coin was eliminated due to capacity constraints, a long parade of Congressionally required programs and the need to concentrate demand on a smaller product-offering list. As long as this remains the case, this coin and all its fractional siblings are highly likely to remain one year type coins.

If the fractional gold Buffalos should ever return to the Mint's offerings they will become members of an ongoing series and will need to compete for supremacy in their denomination's set just as the $50 proof gold Buffalo currently does.

In any event, this very affordable and attractive gold coin is a collector favorite worthy of honorable mention in this or any other moderns listing.

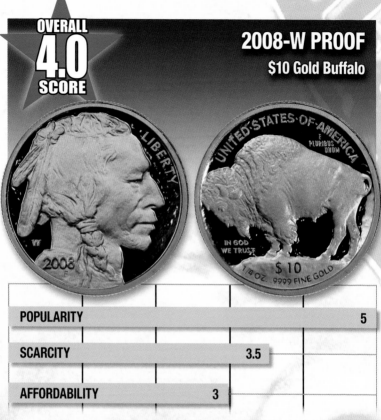

OVERALL 4.0 SCORE

2008-W PROOF
$10 Gold Buffalo

POPULARITY					5
SCARCITY				3.5	
AFFORDABILITY			3		

STATISTICAL INFORMATION

Mintage: 13,125

Obverse Designer: James Earle Fraser

Reverse Designer: James Earle Fraser

Diameter: 22.0 mm

Weight: 7.776 grams

Composition: .9999 gold

AGW: .25 oz.

Edge Type: reeded

ESTIMATED RETAIL VALUE

UNCERTIFIED	NGC PF69 UC	NGC PF70 UC
$1,500	$1,550	$1,800

2008-W Proof
$10 Gold Buffalo

The $10 proof gold Buffalo is becoming very difficult to find in the marketplace because it's attractive to two collector groups.

Classic collectors with an interest in early Buffalo nickels are attracted to this particular denomination because unlike its 2008 siblings, the quarter ounce Buffalo has the correct look and feel of a proof Buffalo nickel struck on gold. Furthermore, there is no such thing as a cameo proof Buffalo nickel even though the Mint sold 10,000 of them in individual packaging.

This 13,125 mintage modern Buffalo can be acquired as a well struck completely bag-mark-free example whose cameo contrast is so strong it looks "gold on black" between the fields and the design's relief. If cameo Buffalo perfection is the goal, this coin is a wonderful option and in some collectors' eyes, the only option.

Another source of demand for this coin is modern Buffalo type collectors. The total denominational mintages of the five-member proof Buffalo type set are show below.

Modern Buffalo Type Set	Total Mintage
2001 Proof $1 Buffalo Silver	272,869
2008-W Proof $5 Buffalo Gold	18,884
2008-W Proof $10 Buffalo Gold	13,125
2008-W Proof $25 Buffalo Gold	12,169
2006-2011 Proof $50 Buffalo Gold	400,000+

Obviously the $10 and $25 denominations are the hardest to find due to dramatically lower mintages than the other siblings. If 12,169 five-coin complete type sets are assembled, that would leave only 956 $10 gold coins to cover the demand from collectors who prefer the classic nickel look. This demand is showing up in the quarter ounce gold coin's price. The $10 proof gold Buffalo has seen its price more than quadruple since 2008, while the $25 gold Buffalo has tripled.

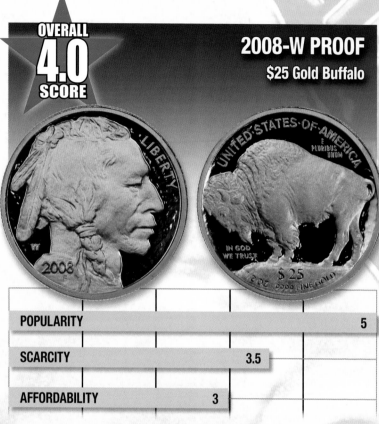

OVERALL 4.0 SCORE

2008-W PROOF
$25 Gold Buffalo

POPULARITY					5
SCARCITY				3.5	
AFFORDABILITY			3		

STATISTICAL INFORMATION

Mintage: 12,169

Obverse Designer: James Earle Fraser

Reverse Designer: James Earle Fraser

Diameter: 26.5 mm

Weight: 15.552 grams

Composition: .9999 gold

AGW: .50 oz.

Edge Type: reeded

ESTIMATED RETAIL VALUE

UNCERTIFIED	NGC PF69 UC	NGC PF70 UC
$1,500	$1,550	$1,900

2008-W Proof
$25 Gold Buffalo

This very attractive and popular coin is the rarest modern proof Buffalo. Like many of the other notable 2008 issues, its scarcity was created by a shortage of coin blanks (planchets), capacity limitations and high scrap rates.

Although 20,602 proof $25 gold Buffalos were struck , only 12,169 made it through quality control into the hands of the public. The Mint, unable to supply silver and Gold Eagle production required by law, did not have time, interest or capacity for low volume programs that were strictly voluntary, so the door on fractional Buffalos was closed leaving this coin and its siblings special one year issues for the foreseeable future.

The Gold Eagles have been a long running and immensely popular series struck on 90 percent coinage gold. The Buffalos are in many ways a competing issue with lower mintages, purer 99.99 percent gold content, and much shorter sets that give the collector lower completion cost. This particular denomination is an extreme example.

The complete 1/2 ounce proof Gold Eagles set is composed of well over 20 Eagles with a total cost over $20,000. The scarcest of the group is the 2008 issue with its 22,602 mintage. The proof gold Buffalo "half type set" has only one member with a 12,169 mintage and costs about $2,000. The collector finds closure quickly and the results are obvious when one looks at the price guide listings. None of the two dozen or so $25 proof Gold Eagles brings anything like the price the lone $25 proof Buffalo does.

Modern Buffalo collectors tend to collect either a type set composed of the five denominations or $50 gold date runs. The type set is listed below.

Proof Buffalos By Type	Total Mintage
2001-P $1 Proof Silver Buffalo	272,869
2008-W $5 Proof Gold Buffalo	18,884
2008-W $10 Proof Gold Buffalo	13,125
2008-W $25 Proof Gold Buffalo	12,169
2006-2012 $50 Proof Gold Buffalo	500,000*

OVERALL
3.5
SCORE

2008-W PROOF
$50 Gold Buffalo

POPULARITY					5
SCARCITY				4	
AFFORDABILITY	2				

STATISTICAL INFORMATION

Mintage: 18,863

Obverse Designer: James Earle Fraser

Reverse Designer: James Earle Fraser

Diameter: 32.7 mm

Weight: 31.103 grams

Composition: .9999 gold

AGW: 1.0 oz.

Edge Type: reeded

ESTIMATED RETAIL VALUE

UNCERTIFIED	NGC PF69 UC	NGC PF70 UC
$3,500	$3,600	$4,750

2008-W Proof
$50 Gold Buffalo

A mintage of 18,863 is not particularly low for modern U.S. gold. Of the eight 2008-W proof and mint state Buffalo issues, the $50 proof is the second most common, but it is easily the most valuable of the eight. While this may seem counter intuitive, there are good reasons for it.

First, when it comes to buying special issues from the Mint at a premium over intrinsic value, the public has a long and clear history of preferring the proof over mint state. This is clearly seen by the fact that proofs typically outsell their mint state siblings by a factor of at least 1.5 to 1, with 3 to 1 being most common.

If a proof's mintage is dramatically higher than its mint state sibling, it can damage the proof's long-term desirability, but if they are close, the proof has the edge.

Second, 2008 is the only year that the $5, $10 and $25 Buffalos were issued, and many collectors who want a four-coin proof gold Buffalo type set want all the coins to be 2008 issues. Thousands of the 2008 $50 coins have been absorbed by four-coin sets so they are not available to assemble proof $50 Buffalo sets.

Lastly, the proof $50 gold Buffalo is the only surviving proof gold Buffalo denomination, so anyone interested in collecting proof Buffalo gold by date has to have this key coin.

The demand for proof $50 gold Buffalos has been deteriorating as is typical for major offerings as they age. Below is a composite graph showing how the average new issue sees its sales drop over time. Sales normally get poorer and poorer until sometime after the fifth year.

The 2008-W proof $50 Buffalo is the third red dot that does not follow the trend line due to the 2008 mintage crash. What we can take away from this is if the price of gold remains stable at its current levels, the 2008-W $50 Buffalo has a fair chance of remaining the lowest mintage date for the foreseeable future.

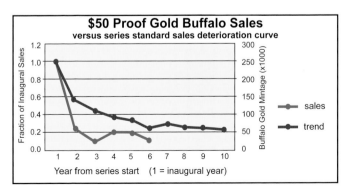

2009 MINT STATE $20
Gold Ultra High Relief

POPULARITY				5
SCARCITY			3	
AFFORDABILITY		2		

STATISTICAL INFORMATION

Mintage: 114,427

Obverse Designer: Augustus Saint-Gaudens

Reverse Designer: Augustus Saint-Gaudens

Diameter: 27.0 mm

Weight: 33.93 grams

Composition: .9167 gold, .03 silver, .0533 copper

AGW: 1.0 oz.

Edge Type: starred

ESTIMATED RETAIL VALUE

UNCERTIFIED	NGC MS69	NGC MS70
$2,850	$3,100	$4,250

2009 Mint State $20
Gold Ultra High Relief

The 2009 mint state $20 gold Ultra High Relief is the ultimate expression of Augustus Saint-Gaudens' original design concept and is considered by many to be the most important accomplishment of the Mint under Director Edmund Moy's tenure.

President Theodore Roosevelt felt that the Barber and Coronet head coinage in circulation in the early 1900s was "atrocious hideousness" and hand picked Saint-Gaudens for the task of redesigning American coinage to fully reflect the greatness of the nation and its ideals, ultimately ushering in a golden age of design excellence.

The $20 Gold Eagle envisioned by Saint-Gaudens was very high relief and struck on a double width $10 gold planchet in order to have enough material thickness to bring out the design. But volume production was impossible. A compromise high relief version was struck under direct instruction of Roosevelt in 1907 with very limited success before a low relief version was forced into service for the rest of the series.

In January 1908, President Roosevelt wrote his friend William Bigelow: "I am very much pleased that you like the coin. ... It is the best coin that has been struck for two thousand years, and no matter what is its temporary fate, it will serve as a model for future coin makers, and eventually the difficulties in connection with making such coins will be surmounted."

It was the Mint's intention to produce the 2009 Ultra High Relief in quantity for only one year resulting in a final mintage of 114,427. Further adding to the interest in the coin, some of them have a proof-like finish that is both hard to find and very desirable.

This coin is not a sub 6,000 mintage modern design-based rarity like many of the coins covered in this text, but that's not necessary for a coin with this kind of collector demand. It is the ultimate expression of the 1986 to present modern Gold Eagles, just as the 1907 high relief gold is the ultimate type coin of the 1907-1933 set.

There are plenty of old "Saints" with lower combined NGC and PCGS populations than the 1907 high relief's roughly 5,000 surviving population, but they don't bring anything like the typical 1907 high relief's $10,000 to $40,000 price tag. We are seeing the same behavior with the 2009 Ultra High Relief, but to a much lesser degree because there are so many more of them.

Master Mintage Listings for First Spouse Gold

First Spouse Gold		
Year	**Proof**	**Mint State**
2007 Washington	19,167	17,661
2007 Adams	17,149	17,142
2007 Jefferson (Liberty)	19,815	19,823
2007 Madison	17,943	12,340
2008 Monroe*	7,800	4,462
2008 Adams	6,581	3,885
2008 Jackson (Liberty)	7,684	4,609
2008 Van Buren (Liberty)	6,807	3,826
2009 Harrison	6,251	3,645
2009 Letitia Tyler	5,296	3,240
2009 Julia Tyler	4,844	3,143
2009 Sarah Polk	5,151	3,489
2009 Margaret Taylor*	4,941	3,629
2010 Fillmore	6,130	3,482
2010 Pierce	4,775	3,338
2010 Buchanan (Liberty)	7,110	5,162
2010 Lincoln*	6,766	3,695

Master Mintage Listings for Buffalo Gold

Mint State Buffalo Gold					Proof Buffalo Gold				
Year	**$50**	**$25**	**$10**	**$5**	**Year**	**$50**	**$25**	**$10**	**$5**
2006	337,012	-	-	-	2006	246,267	-	-	-
2007	136,503	-	-	-	2007	58,998	-	-	-
2008	189,500	-	-	-	2008	18,863	12,169	13,125	18,884
2008-W	9,074	16,908	9,949	17,429	2009	49,306	-	-	-
2009	200,000	-	-	-	2010	49,263	-	-	-
2010	209,000	-	-	-					
2011*	175,000	-	-	-					

These numbers include the final audited data for 2010. The Taylor and Lincoln coins are audited finals as of September 29th of their year of issue but may not include coins sold later in the year therefore they are marked as estimates.

*Estimates

Master Mintage Listings for Mint State Eagles

Mint State Gold Eagles			
Year	$50	$25	$10	$5
1986	1,362,650	599,566	726,031	912,609
1987	1,045,500	131,255	269,255	580,266
1988	465,500	45,000	49,000	159,500
1989	415,790	44,829	81,789	264,790
1990	373,219	31,000	41,000	210,210
1991	243,100	24,100	36,100	165,200
1992	275,000	54,404	59,546	209,300
1993	480,192	73,324	71,864	210,709
1994	221,663	62,400	72,650	206,380
1995	200,636	53,474	83,752	223,025
1996	189,148	39,287	60,318	401,964
1997	664,508	79,605	108,805	528,515
1998	1,468,530	169,029	309,829	1,344,520
1999	1,505,026	263,013	564,232	2,750,338
1999-W	-	-	6,000	6,000*
2000	433,319	79,287	128,964	569,153
2001	143,605	48,047	71,280	269,147
2002	222,029	70,027	62,027	230,027
2003	416,032	79,029	74,029	245,029
2004	417,019	98,040	72,014	250,016
2005	356,555	80,023	72,015	300,043
2006	237,510	66,005	60,004	285,006
2006-W	45,053	15,164	15,188	20,643
2007	140,016	47,002	34,004	190,010
2007-W	18,608	11,455	12,766	22,501
2008	710,000	61,000	70,000	305,000
2008-W	11,908	15,683	8,883	12,657
2009	1,493,000	110,000	110,000	270,000
2010	1,125,000	81,000	86,000	435,000
2011	900,000	65000	82,000	370,000*
2011-W	8,800	-	-	-*

*Estimates

Master Mintage Listings for Mint State Eagles

Business Strike Platinum Eagles

Year	$100	$50	$25	$10
1997 Eagle Over the Sun	56,000	20,500	27,100	70,250
1998 Eagle Over the Sun	133,002	32,419	38,887	39,525
1999 Eagle Over the Sun	56,707	32,309	39,734	55,955
2000 Eagle Over the Sun	10,003	18,892	20,054	34,027
2001 Eagle Over the Sun	14,070	12,815	21,815	52,017
2002 Eagle Over the Sun	11,502	24,005	27,405	23,005
2003 Eagle Over the Sun	8,007	17,409	25,207	22,007
2004 Eagle Over the Sun	7,009	13,236	18,010	15,010
2005 Eagle Over the Sun	6,310	9,013	12,013	14,013
2006 Eagle Over the Sun	6,000	9,602	12,001	11,001
2007 Eagle Over the Sun	7,202	7,001	8,402	13,003
2008 Eagle Over the Sun	21,800	14,000	22,800	17,000

Changing Reverse Mint State Platinum Eagles

Year	$100	$50	$25	$10
2006-W Legislative	3,068	2,577	2,676	3,544
2007-W Executive	4,177	3,635	3,690	5,556
2008-W Judicial	2,876	2,253	2,481	3,706

Mint State Silver Eagles

Year	$1	Year	$1	Year	$1
1986	5,393,005	1997	4,295,004	2007	9,028,036
1987	11,442,335	1998	4,847,547	2007 W	690,891
1988	5,004,646	1999	7,408,640	2008	20,583,000
1989	5,203,327	2000	9,239,132	2008 W*	535,000
1990	5,840,110	2001	9,001,711	2008 W 07 reverse	< 46,318
1991	7,191,066	2002	10,539,026	2009	30,459,500
1992	5,540,068	2003	8,495,008	2009	30,459,500
1993	6,763,762	2004	8,882,754	2010	34,764,500
1994	4,227,319	2005	8,891,025	2011*	40,000,000
1995	4,672,051	2006	10,676,522	2011-S*	100,000
1996	3,603,386	2006 W	466,573	2011-W*	400,000

Estimates

Master Mintage Listings for Proof Eagles

Proof Platinum Eagles

Year/Reverse Design	$100	$50	$25	$10
1997 Eagle Over Sun	20,851	15,431	18,628	36,993
1998 New England	14,912	13,836	14,873	19,847
1999 Wet Lands	12,363	11,103	13,507	19,133
2000 Heart Land	12,453	11,049	11,995	15,651
2001 South West	8,969	8,254	8,847	12,174
2002 North West	9,834	8,772	9,282	12,365
2003 Patriotic Vigilance	8,246	7,131	7,044	9,534
2004 Seated America	6,007	5,063	5,193	7,161
2005 Plenty	6,602	5,942	6,592	8,104
2006 Legislative	9,152	7,649	7,813	10,205
2007 Executive	8,363	22,873	6,017	8,176
2007 Reverse Proof	-	16,937	-	-
2008 Judicial	4,769	4,020	4,153	5,138
2009 Perfect Union	7,945	-	-	-
2010 Establish Justice	9,871	-	-	-
2011 Domestic Tranquility*	15,000	-	-	-

Proof Gold Eagles

Year	$50	$25	$10	$5
1986	446,290	-	-	-
1987	147,498	143,398	-	-
1988	87,133	76,528	98,028	143,881
1989	54,570	44,798	54,170	84,647
1990	62,401	51,636	62,674	99,349
1991	50,411	53,125	50,839	70,334
1992	44,826	40,976	46,269	64,874
1993	34,369	31,130	33,775	45,960
1994	46,674	44,584	48,172	62,849
1995	46,368	45,388	47,526	62,667
1996	36,153	35,058	38,219	57,047
1997	28,034	26,344	29,805	34,977
1998	25,886	25,374	29,503	39,395
1999	31,427	30,427	34,417	48,428
2000	33,007	32,028	36,036	49,971
2001	24,555	23,240	25,613	37,530
2002	27,499	26,646	29,242	40,864
2003	28,344	28,270	30,292	40,027
2004	28,215	27,330	28,839	35,131
2005	35,246	34,311	37,207	49,265
2006	47,000	34,322	36,127	47,277
2006 Rev. Proof	9,996	-	-	-
2007	51,810	44,025	46,189	58,553
2008	30,237	22,602	18,877	28,116
2009	-	-	-	-
2010	59,480	44,527	44,507	44,285

Data is final for 2010

Proof Silver Eagles

Year	$1
1986	1,446,778
1987	904,732
1988	557,370
1989	617,694
1990	695,510
1991	511,924
1992	498,543
1993	405,913
1994	372,168
1995	407,822
1995-W	30,102
1996	498,293
1997	440,315
1998	450,728
1999	549,330
2000	600,743
2001	746,398
2002	647,342
2003	747,831
2004	801,602
2005	816,663
2006	1,092,475
2006 Rev Pf	248,875
2007	821,759
2008	700,979
2009	-
2010	849,861
2011*	950,000
2011 Rev Pf*	100,000

*Estimates

Top 50 Modern Coins Checklist

- ☐ 2007 Mint State $1 George Washington Presidential Dollar Mint Error Missing Edge Lettering
- ☐ 2001-D Mint State $1 Silver Buffalo Commemorative
- ☐ 2001-P Proof $1 Silver Buffalo Commemorative
- ☐ 1997-W Mint State $5 Gold Jackie Robinson Commemorative
- ☐ 1997-W Proof $5 Gold Jackie Robinson Commemorative
- ☐ 2000-W Mint State $10 Bi-Metallic Library of Congress Commemorative
- ☐ 2000-W Proof $10 Bi-Metallic Library of Congress Commemorative
- ☐ 2007-W Mint State $10 First Spouse Gold Thomas Jefferson's Liberty
- ☐ 2007-W Proof $10 First Spouse Gold Thomas Jefferson's Liberty
- ☐ 2008-W Mint State $10 First Spouse Gold Andrew Jackson's Liberty
- ☐ 2008-W Proof $10 First Spouse Gold Andrew Jackson's Liberty
- ☐ 2008-W Mint State $10 First Spouse Gold Martin Van Buren's Liberty
- ☐ 2008-W Proof $10 First Spouse Gold Martin Van Buren's Liberty
- ☐ 2010-W Mint State $10 First Spouse Gold James Buchanan's Liberty
- ☐ 2010-W Proof $10 First Spouse Gold James Buchanan's Liberty
- ☐ 1995-W Proof 10th Anniversary $1 Silver Eagle
- ☐ 2006-P Reverse Proof 20th Anniversary $1 Silver Eagle
- ☐ 2006-W Mint State Burnished $1 Silver Eagle
- ☐ 2008-W Mint State Burnished $1 Silver Eagle Reverse of 2007
- ☐ 2011-P Reverse Proof 25th Anniversary $1 Silver Eagle
- ☐ 2011-S Mint State 25th Anniversary $1 Silver Eagle
- ☐ 1999-W Mint State Unfinished Proof Dies $5 Gold Eagle
- ☐ 1999-W Mint State Unfinished Proof Dies $10 Gold Eagle
- ☐ 2006-W Reverse Proof 20th Anniversary $50 Gold Eagle
- ☐ 2008-W Mint State Burnished $5 Gold Eagle
- ☐ 2008-W Mint State Burnished $10 Gold Eagle
- ☐ 2008-W Mint State Burnished $25 Gold Eagle
- ☐ 2008-W Mint State Burnished $50 Gold Eagle
- ☐ 2004-W Proof $10 Platinum Eagle
- ☐ 2004-W Proof $25 Platinum Eagle
- ☐ 2004-W Proof $50 Platinum Eagle
- ☐ 2004-W Proof $100 Platinum Eagle
- ☐ 2006-W Mint State Burnished $10 Platinum Eagle
- ☐ 2006-W Mint State Burnished $25 Platinum Eagle
- ☐ 2006-W Mint State Burnished $50 Platinum Eagle
- ☐ 2006-W Mint State Burnished $100 Platinum Eagle
- ☐ 2007-W Reverse Proof 10th Anniversary $50 Platinum Eagle
- ☐ 2008-W Mint State Burnished $10 Platinum Eagle
- ☐ 2008-W Mint State Burnished $25 Platinum Eagle
- ☐ 2008-W Mint State Burnished $50 Platinum Eagle
- ☐ 2008-W Mint State Burnished $100 Platinum Eagle
- ☐ 2008-W Mint State $5 Gold Buffalo
- ☐ 2008-W Mint State $10 Gold Buffalo
- ☐ 2008-W Mint State $25 Gold Buffalo
- ☐ 2008-W Mint State $50 Gold Buffalo
- ☐ 2008-W Proof $5 Gold Buffalo
- ☐ 2008-W Proof $10 Gold Buffalo
- ☐ 2008-W Proof $25 Gold Buffalo
- ☐ 2008-W Proof $50 Gold Buffalo
- ☐ 2009 Mint State $20 Gold Ultra High Relief